That's Really Funny!

Over 1,000 More Great Jokes from Today's Hottest Comedians

MJF BOOKS
NEW YORK

Published by MJF Books
Fine Communications
Two Lincoln Square
60 West 66th Street
New York, NY 10023

That's Really Funny!
Library of Congress Control No. 2001090533
ISBN 1-56731-468-6

Manufactured in the United States of America on acid-free paper ∞

MJF Books and the MJF colophon are trademarks of Fine Creative Media, Inc.

MV   10   9   8   7   6   5   4   3   2   1

Contents

There is a very fine line between "hobby" and "mental illness."
—DAVE BARRY

I don't care about money. I want a sensitive man. I want a man who will cry when I hit him.
—WENDY LIEBMAN

Men like to barbecue.
Men will cook if
danger is involved.
—RITA RUDNER

My grandfather invented
Cliffs Notes. It all started
back in 1912. . . . Well, to
make a long story short . . .
—STEVEN WRIGHT

That's Really Funny!

Everything's Relative

Dad

You know when, like, you're little, your dad, you think he's Superman. Then you grow up and you realize he's just a regular guy who wears a cape. —DAVE ATTELL

To be fair to my father, he did hug me once on my twenty-first birthday. It was very awkward, and I think I know what it was that made me feel so uncomfortable . . . the nudity. —RAY ROMANO

Listen up, fathers: If you want to mistreat your young daughter, congratulations. You'll be seeing her in a porn movie later on. —ADAM CORROLLA

My dad was always on the run from the cops, and I never saw him out of disguise until I was twenty-two. For years, I thought he was a short, bearded man with dark glasses and a limp. —WOODY ALLEN

Dad taught me all I know about remodeling by making an example of our house. Our house was like one of the great European cathedrals: never finished.
—MICHAEL FELDMAN

Having me for a dad is kind of like having Curly from the Three Stooges as your father. —BOBCAT GOLDTHWAIT

When I was little, my grandfather
used to make me stand in a closet for
five minutes without moving.
He said it was elevator practice.

—STEVEN WRIGHT

Since Dad was a CPA, during tax season we hardly saw him at all. In fact, he almost didn't see me, born as I was on March 14, one day before the old filing deadline. I do seem to remember somebody popping in with ledgers under his arms, but it may have just been birth stress. —MICHAEL FELDMAN

My father was fired. He worked for the same firm for twelve years. They replaced him with a tiny gadget that does everything that my father does, only it does it much better. The depressing thing is, my mother ran out and bought one. —WOODY ALLEN

My grandfather gave me a watch. It doesn't have any hands or numbers. He says it's very accurate. I asked him what time it was. You can guess what he told me. —STEVEN WRIGHT

Fathers are the geniuses of the house.
We're the geniuses of the house because
only a person intelligent as we
could fake such stupidity.
—BILL COSBY

My grandfather invented *Cliffs Notes*. It all started back in 1912. . . . Well, to make a long story short . . .
—STEVEN WRIGHT

Mom

My mother loves to clean. She'll say, "Look at this. You could eat off my floor." You could eat off my floor, too. There are thousands of things down there.
—ELAYNE BOOSLER

My mother used to tell me things. She had natural childbirth. I recently found out it was her version of natural childbirth. She took off her makeup. —RITA RUDNER

As a mom, I'd hate to hear "Mom, who do you love most?" Because then I'd have to say, "You know, I never wanted children." —LAURA KIGHTLINGER

My mom's a ventriloquist. Can you believe that? She can throw her voice. So for, like, ten years, I thought the dog was telling me to kill my father. I got my brother to do it. —WENDY LIEBMAN

My mother loves tranquilizers; she thinks they're the best things that have ever been invented. I'm not talking about, like, Prozac, no; to my mother, Prozac is like Tic Tacs. I mean, she's using, like, horse tranquilizers; you know, the kind they use in the circus. That's where she gets them. She pulls up to a tent, and a clown comes out and hands her a bag.
—FRANK MAYA

This is as mad as my mother ever got: "Y'all quit. Don't make me stop this car." "Mama, you're not in the car, you're in the hammock with a jelly jar full of Scotch." Then she'd say, "Wait till your father gets home." "Mama, it's been eight years." —BRETT BUTLER

I'm very loyal in relationships. Even when I go out with my mom, I don't look at other moms. —GARRY SHANDLING

Growing up, my mom used to bust at me; she said to me, "You keep wearing those boxer shorts, your thing's gonna hang down to your knee." "So what's the downside to your argument here?" What a liar Mom turned out to be, too.
—JEFF FOXWORTHY

My mother always said don't marry for money, divorce for money. —WENDY LIEBMAN

My grandmother was a very tough woman. She buried three husbands. Two of them were just napping.
—RITA RUDNER

The most remarkable thing about my mother is that for thirty years, she served the family nothing but leftovers. The original meal has never been found.
—CALVIN TRILLIN

My ex-boyfriend's mother told me she felt my material was men-bashing, and that I hate men. I said, "I don't hate all men, just your son. That's just one guy."
—LAURA KIGHTLINGER

Don't get me wrong. I support whatever your sexual preference as long as you're committed. I myself can't believe eventually I will have to marry someone the same sex as my mother. —GARRY SHANDLING

My mother used to say to me when I was younger, "If a strange man comes up to you, and offers you candy, and wants you to get into the back of his car with him . . . go."
—WOODY ALLEN

I'll be a really good mother. I've been called one. I'll be really overprotective. I won't let the kid outside. Of my body. —WENDY LIEBMAN

Baby Days

I wonder what our children would be like. My husband is English and I'm American. They'd probably be rude but disgusted by their behavior. —RITA RUDNER

Never tell a woman that you didn't realize she was pregnant unless you're certain that she is.
—DAVE BARRY

> I would like to have kids one day, but I only have one egg left. Uh-oh, there it went, sorry. I'm ovulating right now.
> —CATHY LADMAN

Advice to expectant mothers: You must remember that when you are pregnant, you are eating for two. But you must also remember that the other one of you is about the size of a golf ball, so let's not go overboard with it. I mean, a lot of pregnant women eat as though the other person they're eating for is Orson Welles. —DAVE BARRY

Childbirth is a miracle. No, it's not. . . . It's a chemical reaction, that's all. Raisin' a kid that doesn't talk in a movie theater. Okay, there is a goddamn miracle. It's not a miracle if every nine months any yin-yang in the world can drop a litter of mewling cabbages on our planet. And just in case you haven't seen the single-mom statistics lately, the miracle is spreading like wildfire. —BILL HICKS

A twenty-eight-year-old woman who was stuck in traffic gave birth to a baby on the Long Island Expressway.

Afterwards, the young mother said, "It was very touching. Several other motorists celebrated by beeping their horns and giving us the finger." —CONAN O'BRIEN

I would like to wear my fallopian tubes on the outside, 'cause they're so pretty.
—CATHY LADMAN

My wife wanted me to videotape the birth of the baby. That's sick. You know, being there was hard enough. I believe that all men should be there. That's something you must experience. Everyone should be there, just don't watch. —DAMON WAYANS

If a woman has to choose between catching a fly ball and saving an infant's life, she will choose to save the infant's life without even considering if there are men on base. —DAVE BARRY

We had a C-section. That's when the baby comes out like toast. —BOBCAT GOLDTHWAIT

The old system of having a baby was much better than the new system, the old system being characterized by the fact that the man didn't have to watch. —DAVE BARRY

My friend has a baby. I'm recording all the noises he makes so later I can ask him what he meant. —STEVEN WRIGHT

My friend has a sixteen-month-old. The baby's crawling around and he has an accident in his diaper. . . . And the mother comes over and says, "Isn't that adorable? Brandon made a gift for Daddy." I'm thinking this guy must be real easy to shop for on Father's Day.
—GARRY SHANDLING

My sister had a baby, and I was watching her breast-feed for a couple of bucks. . . . —DAVE ATTELL

For most of history, baby-having was in the hands (so to speak) of women. Many fine people were born under this system. Things changed in the 1970s. The birthrate dropped sharply. Women started going to college and driving bulldozers and carrying briefcases and using words like *debenture*. They didn't have time to have babies. . . . Then young professional couples began to realize that their lives were missing something: a sense of stability, of companionship, of responsibility for another life. So they got Labrador retrievers. A little later, they started having babies again, mainly because of the tax advantages. —DAVE BARRY

Babies don't need vacations, but I still see them at the beach. —STEVEN WRIGHT

Hi, I'm Bill. I'm a birth survivor.

—BILL MAHER

Family

I've thought about having a family. I just haven't seen any that really appeal to me. —LAURA KIGHTLINGER

Remember that three out of four homicide victims are killed by a spouse, family member, friend, or acquaintance. Which is comforting for all of us who fear random violence. —AL FRANKEN

If your family tree does not fork,
you might be a redneck.

—JEFF FOXWORTHY

I've got stepcousins. Think about it—stepcousins—as if cousins aren't worthless enough as it is. Stepcousins—I don't know what to do with these people. I'm not blood-related to them; the only thing I can think of is it's okay to have sex with them. In fact, I don't even go to singles bars anymore; I'm just waiting for Thanksgiving.
—JUDD APATOW

I just spent three days with my family. Out on Long Island, we had a family reunion. I had to take the Long Island Rail Road, got stuck in the child-beating car.
—FRANK MAYA

Parents and Parenting

My parents are what you would call "old-world." They're very stable, down-to-earth people. They don't believe in divorce. Their values are God and carpeting.
—WOODY ALLEN

Ask your child what he wants for dinner only if he's buying.
—FRAN LEBOWITZ

I have nephews. . . . I remember the first time they stayed with us. My sister-in-law, she calls me—it was after midnight—and she's, like, "Did you have a hard time getting the boys to sleep?" I'm, like, "Sleep? Girl, we sitting up drinking liquor playing Nintendo."
—WANDA SYKES-HALL

Never raise your hands to your kids.
It leaves your groin unprotected.
—RED BUTTONS

I did get even with my parents. My parents came to stay with me for the weekend in my apartment. You know what I did? I made 'em sleep in separate bedrooms. My mother said "What, are you crazy? I've been sleeping with this man for years." I said, "Look, I don't care what you do on the outside, but when you're in my house . . ."
—ELAYNE BOOSLER

We're trying to bring them up the right way. We're not spanking them. We find that we don't have to spank them. We find that waving the guns around pretty much gets the job done. —DENIS LEARY

We've been married six years, so people trying to force us to have kids; it's like we're cheating or something. . . . They all say the same thing: "Kids—they a lot of work, but they worth it." But I noticed something. They never look you in the eye when they say that.

—WANDA SYKES-HALL

Getting down on all fours and imitating a rhinoceros stops babies from crying. (Put an empty cigarette pack on your nose for a horn and make loud "snort" noises.) I don't know why parents don't do this more often. Usually it makes the kid laugh. Sometimes it sends him into shock. Either way, it quiets him down. If you're a parent, acting like a rhino has another advantage. Keep it up until the kid is a teenager, and he definitely won't have his friends hanging around your house all the time.

—P. J. O'ROURKE

You get a lot of tension. You get a lot of headaches. I do what it says on the aspirin bottle: Take two and keep away from children. —ROSEANNE

Even very young children need to be informed about dying. Explain the concept of death very carefully to your child. This will make threatening him with it much more effective. —P. J. O'ROURKE

My parent's used to stuff me with candy when I was little—all this candy. M&M's, jujubees, Sweetarts. I don't think they wanted a child. I think they wanted a piñata. I hated that stick. —WENDY LIEBMAN

My parents were both cheap. I'm sure that's why they got married in the first place. They weren't in love. They just realized, "We could save a lot of money if we was together."
—CHRIS ROCK

My parents used to take me to Lewis' department store in Glasgow. They were skinflints. They used to take me to the pet department and tell me it was the zoo.
—BILLY CONNOLLY

> If you are truly serious about preparing
> your child for the future, don't teach him
> to subtract, teach him to deduct.
> —FRAN LEBOWITZ

We have some really bad children's books on our shelves because I often take the kids with me to the bookstore, and I have shamelessly judged books by their covers in my haste to get out of the store before one of the kids drools on an atlas or runs amock in the self-help section. —PAULA POUNDSTONE

I know I want to have children while my parents are still young enough to take care of them. —RITA RUDNER

The only real joy I'm having in not having any children is that it's driving my parents crazy, and I really like that a lot. I feel like I'm getting even for all those years in high school when they made me come home early so I couldn't have sex. —ELAYNE BOOSLER

One thing they never tell you about child raising is that for the rest of your life, at the drop of a hat, you are expected to know your child's name and how old he or she is. —ERMA BOMBECK

Everyone who ever walked barefoot into his child's room late at night hates LEGOs. —TONY KORNHEISER

I was in analysis for years. I had
a traumatic childhood.
I was breast-fed from falsies.
—WOODY ALLEN

I figure that if the children are alive when my husband gets home, I've done my job. —ROSEANNE

Halcyon Days

How can any child resist the tooth fairy? That single shining example of selfless generosity in this slimy veil of greed in which we live. I remember when I was broke, I used to pull out my brother's teeth. Not every day . . . I mean, you couldn't make a living at it, but just to know it was there . . . for an emergency. That was enough. Naturally, it was too good to last. It was just one more nonrenewable resource on a diminishing planet. —A. WHITNEY BROWN

When I was a little kid, we had a sandbox. It was a quicksand box. I was an only child . . . eventually.
—STEVEN WRIGHT

People think living in your parents' basement until you're twenty-nine is lame. But what they don't realize is that while you're there, you save money on rent, food, and dates. —RAY ROMANO

When you're a kid, it's so easy to have fun. What do you need? A book of matches, some oily rags, a little brother?
—DAVE ATTELL

The Little Dears

Children make the most desirable opponents in Scrabble, as they are both easy to beat and fun to cheat.
—FRAN LEBOWITZ

Kids are great. I love kids! You know that look in a child's eye when you take him out of your trunk?
—DAVE ATTELL

Even when freshly washed and relieved of all obvious confections, children tend to be sticky.
—FRAN LEBOWITZ

What's harder to raise, boys or girls?
Girls. Who said boys? Boys are easy.
Give 'em a book of matches and
they're happy.
—ETTA MAY

Notoriously insensitive to subtle shifts in mood, children will persist in discussing the color of a recently sighted cement-mixer long after one's own interest in the topic has waned. —FRAN LEBOWITZ

I baby-sit for my best friend's
three-year-old. I mean, don't kids say the
darnedest things? When they're drunk?
—WENDY LIEBMAN

Children are usually small in stature, which makes them quite useful for getting at those hard-to-reach places.
—FRAN LEBOWITZ

A new study shows that fewer and fewer kids are bringing guns to school. Apparently, a lot of kids have been using the old excuse, "My dog ate my ammo."
—CONAN O'BRIEN

Never allow your child to call you by your first name. He hasn't known you long enough.
—FRAN LEBOWITZ

The Opposites of Sex

Can You Relate?

You know, when you get back together with an old boyfriend, it's pathetic. It's like having a garage sale and buying your own stuff back. —LAURA KIGHTLINGER

There is one thing I would break up over, and that is if she caught me with another woman. I won't stand for that. —STEVE MARTIN

If you're a guy, you have absolutely no idea what's going on at any time in the relationship, ever. Here's what you know: You know when you're getting laid, and you know when it's all over. Those are the only two things you're aware of.
—ADAM CORROLLA

Getting rid of a man without hurting his masculinity is a problem. "Get out and I never want to see you again" might sound like a challenge. If you want to get rid of a man, I suggest saying, "I love you. . . . I want to marry you. . . . I want to have your children." Sometimes they leave skid marks. —RITA RUDNER

I go to couples therapy. I go alone.
There are two therapists.
—GARRY SHANDLING

Starting a relationship is like buying a cellular phone:
They let you in real easy. You can get one real cheap.
But one day, that bill will bust your ass. —CHRIS ROCK

I feel bad sometimes 'cause I'm still in bad relationships,
and all my friends are already headlong into bad marriages. —LAURA KIGHTLINGER

Just 'cause you look at another woman, if you're a
woman and you look at another man, it doesn't mean
you are going to do anything. I mean, you are at a
restaurant and food comes to another table, you might
look at it. It doesn't mean you are gonna dive in and
start eating it. It's not like I look at another woman and
turn to my girlfriend and say, "I wish I got that. Why
didn't I get what he's having?" —GARRY SHANDLING

Dated

I don't go out with my single friends, not at all. 'Cause I
never have a good time. Never have fun. We go to a

club; guy comes over. "Hey, can I buy you a drink?" They're like, "Uh-uh, no, no, she married." "Yeah, I'm married, but I'm thirsty. Why don't you shut the hell up and let me have a free drink?" —**WANDA SYKES-HALL**

What would the world be like if people said whatever they were thinking, all the time, whenever it came to them? How long would a blind date last? About thirteen seconds, I think. "Oh, sorry, your rear end is too big." "That's okay; your breath stinks, anyway. See you later."

—**JERRY SEINFELD**

We men are driven to meet Miss Right . . . or at least Miss Right Now. —**ROBIN WILLIAMS**

Younger guys have been approaching me lately. And asking me to buy their alcohol. —**WENDY LIEBMAN**

Single people probably have the toughest life. Just the word *single* itself: S I N G L E: *S*tay *I*ntoxicated *N*ightly; *G*et *L*aid *E*very day. —**JEFF FOXWORTHY**

If you're dating a man who you think might be "Mr. Right," if he (a) got older, (b) got a new job, or (c) visited a psychiatrist, you are in for a nasty surprise. The cocoon-to-butterfly theory only works on cocoons and butterflies. —RITA RUDNER

I don't care about money. I want a sensitive man. I want a man who will cry when I hit him. —WENDY LIEBMAN

My friends actually set me up on blind dates. Now I know why they call them blind dates. When you see the girl, you want to jab something sharp into your eyeballs. —KEVIN MEANEY

Single people throw the best parties. They don't have to worry about their furniture getting messed up. Their friends can destroy everything they own. They're out fifteen bucks. —JEFF FOXWORTHY

Dating means doing a lot of fun things you will never do again if you get married. The fun stops with marriage because you're trying to save money for when you split up your property. —DAVE BARRY

I turned down a date once because I was looking for someone a little closer to the top of the food chain. —JUDY TENUTA

Two of my old boyfriends are gay. Should I feel weird about that? Gosh, it's like they were going, "Gosh, I'd really like to go out with a guy, but I'm just not ready to take that leap; oh, Sue Murphy's available, perfect." The only reason I mention that, is that if there's anyone out there feeling remotely attracted to me, you're probably gay.
—SUE MURPHY

Have you ever dated someone because you were too lazy to commit suicide? —JUDY TENUTA

I got dumped on New Year's Eve; this is so lame. I was going out with this guy that I was really crazy about, and he did that thing where halfway through the relationship he ripped the mask off and changed personalities. —KATHY GRIFFIN

I was on a date with this really hot model. . . . Just play along, all right? —DAVE ATTELL

Never let a fool kiss you, or a kiss fool you.
—JOEY ADAMS

If I ever got money, I would open a restaurant for single people. And I'd make 'em feel comfortable, too. Name it Just One. You walk in, nice long row of sinks. No tables and chairs. Everybody eats standing over the sink. All the food comes in the package, so you can read the back while you're eating. —ELAYNE BOOSLER

When I'm not in a relationship, I shave one leg so when I sleep, it feels like I'm with a woman.
—GARRY SHANDLING

A man who was loved by three hundred women singled me out to live with him. Why? I was the only one without a cat. —ELAYNE BOOSLER

I met this wonderful girl at Macy's. She was buying clothes, and I was putting Slinkys on the escalator.

—STEVEN WRIGHT

A hat should be taken off when you greet a lady and left off for the rest of your life. Nothing looks more stupid than a hat. —P. J. O'ROURKE

I wear my heart on my sleeve. I wear my liver on my pant leg. —STEVEN WRIGHT

If love is the answer, could you please rephrase the question? —LILY TOMLIN

Let's Talk about Sex

Someone asked me once, "If you had a girlfriend, would you keep it quiet?" And I told them, "No, I would rent that Times Square billboard thing and put out GUESS WHO'S GETTING LAID? in big, bold neon letters and flash it at the crowd." —JON STEWART

I'd like to die while making love—that would be great—but after the orgasm. It would be terrible to die before the orgasm. I'd be up in Heaven; people would be pointing at me. "Oh, she looks so tense. Somebody should send her back, for, like, an hour." —CATHY LADMAN

Some people say, "I like women to talk dirty during sex." I like them to shut up; I'm trying to last a decent time. —BILLY CONNOLLY

I was great in bed last night. I never once had to sit up and consult the manual.

—WOODY ALLEN

I used to think a condom was enough protection. I'm starting to wear The Club. —GARRY SHANDLING

Before sleeping together today, people should boil themselves. —RICHARD LEWIS

They won't advertise condoms on network TV 'cause it'll lead young people to have sex. Like beer isn't the leading cause of sex amongst young people. How many people here have ever gotten laid because they had too many condoms at a party one night?

—JON STEWART

When the clerk tried to sell me condoms that were made of sheep intestines because they have a more natural feel, I said, "Not for northern women."

—ELAYNE BOOSLER

I don't even masturbate anymore, I'm so afraid I'll give myself something. I just want to be friends with myself.
—RICHARD LEWIS

There's a new medical crisis. Doctors are reporting that many men are having allergic reactions to latex condoms. They say they cause severe swelling. So what's the problem? —JAY LENO

American sex shops are the most bizarre. They sell these inflatable dolls, but they also sell just the head—supposedly for people to drive along the freeway with.
—BILLY CONNOLLY

In 1962, the expression "safe sex," all that meant then was you just move the bed from against the wall so you won't bang your head. —DAVID LETTERMAN

My wife and I had an airbag installed on the headboard of our bed, and I'm firmly convinced it saved my life.
—DENNIS MILLER

To a man, sex is like a car accident, and determining a female orgasm is like being asked, "What did you see after the car went out of control?" "Well, I remember I heard a lot of screeching noises. I was facing the wrong way at one point, and in the end, my body was thrown clear." —JERRY SEINFELD

A psychiatrist told me and my wife we should have sex every night; now we'll never see each other.
—RODNEY DANGERFIELD

Sex is not easy. Women have two types of orgasms. The actual one and the ones that they make up on their own. I can give you the male point of view on this, which is, we're fine with it. You do whatever the hell you gotta do. —JERRY SEINFELD

I was involved in an extremely good example of oral contraception two weeks ago. I asked a girl to go to bed with me, and she said no. —WOODY ALLEN

Last time I tried to make love to my wife, nothing was happening, so I said to her, "What's the matter? You can't think of anybody, either?" —RODNEY DANGERFIELD

When I have sex, it takes four minutes. And that includes dinner and a show. —GILBERT GOTTFRIED

I have not had sex in almost two years, and I think once you hit two years, you automatically get your virginity back. You get to start over, and I'm about to. What is wrong with me? I don't understand. I'm just going to have to trick somebody into doing it. Use trickery. I'm going to have to cover myself with leaves and hope somebody falls in. —MARGARET CHO

I'm afraid to give instructions in bed because I'm afraid I'll get carried away. "Okay, pull my hair, and touch me right there. No, to the left. Now go outside and move my car so I won't get a ticket. Yeah, that's it."
—LAURA KIGHTLINGER

New research shows that the more sex a man has, the more he wants. Not only that, the research also shows the less sex a man has, the more he wants.
—CONAN O'BRIEN

What's the number-one fantasy for most guys? Two women, two girls. . . . That's what they want—two women. Fellows, I think that's a bit lofty. 'Cause, come on, think about it; if you can't satisfy that one woman, why you wanna piss off another one? —WANDA SYKES-HALL

Scientists announced that they've located the gene for intelligence. When they found it, it was downloading porn off the Internet. —CONAN O'BRIEN

The cable TV sex channels don't expand our horizons, don't make us better people, and don't come in clearly enough. —BILL MAHER

Casual sex is the best, because you don't have to wear a tie. —JOHN MENDOZA

Comedy is like sex. The more noise you hear, the better you think you're doing. —RAY ROMANO

According to a new poll, 82 percent of Americans are in favor of sex education in the schools. The other 18 percent prefer the old-fashioned way—outside the school behind the Dumpster. —JAY LENO

Love is the answer, but while you are waiting for the answer, sex raises some pretty good questions.
—WOODY ALLEN

Seems to me the basic conflict between men and women, sexually, is that men are like firemen. To us, sex is an emergency, and no matter what we're doing, we can be ready in two minutes. Women, on the other

hand, are like fire. They're very exciting, but the conditions have to be exactly right for it to occur.
—JERRY SEINFELD

Kinky sex involves the use of duck feathers. Perverted sex involves the whole duck.

—LEWIS GRIZZARD

A new cologne is coming out. It's for cowboys, and it's made from cow manure. That way, the women will be on you like flies. —BILL MAHER

Scientists say they have now developed a pill that will cure baldness, but one of the side effects of the pill is impotence. That's irony, isn't it? Now you can get the girl, but you can't do anything with her! —JAY LENO

Every X-rated movie should be called what it is—*Shit That Never Happens to You, Ever.* —RICHARD JENI

I mean, let's face it; everyone wants a prostitute, but you want them the first day on the job.
—KATHY GRIFFIN

I'm just a huge fan of the penis. Can I just say I just love penises? They're just the greatest. And they're all different, like snowflakes. —MARGARET CHO

Of course, I want to have sex with teenaged girls. Doesn't everyone? That's why there's a law. What do you think, they pulled eighteen out of a hat?
—MARC MARON

I love a mirror during sex! I like to look at myself and say, "Hey, look who's getting laid!" Then I high-five my reflection and break the glass. —ADAM CORROLLA

Some people have a mirror above the bed to watch themselves doing it. But I'm such an ugly bastard, I don't want to see a big white arse moving up and down.
—BILLY CONNOLLY

The difference between sex and death is that with death, you can do it alone and no one is going to make fun of you. —WOODY ALLEN

My friend brought me to a strip bar in L.A. —this is recently—and I got a table dance. This is where a woman dances naked for you right in front of you. I had never had one before this point, and I didn't know how to behave. I mean, what's proper etiquette during a table dance? Are you just supposed to sit there and say, "Hey"? —MARC MARON

I've thought, "What would I want in the perfect woman?" And I think it would have to be a penis. —SUE MURPHY

The vagina is the strongest muscle in the human body. Think about it this way: A strong man can lift things like a couch, but the vagina will make you buy the couch. —DAVE ATTELL

My husband never said I wasn't good, but I could tell. I said to him once, "Why don't you call out my name when we're making love?" He said, "I don't want to wake you up." —JOAN RIVERS

The last woman I had sex with just hated me. I could tell by the way she asked for the money. —DREW CAREY

You spend a whole night naked with somebody with every part of your body. Doing things the Flying Wallendas wouldn't do with clothing on. And then you wake up in the morning and you won't use their toothbrush. Whaddya thinking? "Well, the sun's up; I have morals again." —ELAYNE BOOSLER

Latin men are incredibly noisy in bed. I had no idea that there were even that many saints. Oh my goodness.
—CAROLINE RHEA

Luckily sex isn't that important to me. You know what's important to me? That afterwards part. You know when you're both naked and it's warm and you're watching the sun come up through the windshield and you hear those magic words: "Let the girl go." —DAVE ATTELL

Men are very sweet, they like to hold you the whole night. It's not comfortable. I think you should make love and go to your corners. This holding thing, it's like Marxism. It works well in theory, not in practice.
—ELAYNE BOOSLER

I think I'd be really hot if I didn't talk. That's my problem. I just have a big mouth, and I just say the wrong things, but I don't know. It's weird; I try. I have one pick-up line which never works. This is what I do: If I'm at a club and I see a guy that I like, I smile, and if he smiles back, I feel comfortable, and when I feel really comfortable, I'll walk over and I'll say, "Stick it in!"
—MARGARET CHO

I am relaxed tonight. I just discovered an alternate use for my shower massage. —BRETT BUTLER

Then Comes Marriage

After fifteen minutes, I wanted to marry her, and after thirty minutes, I completely gave up the idea of stealing her purse. —WOODY ALLEN

Eventually in your life, you have to get married. You just have to. That's probably what I'll say at the ceremony: "I'll go; I have to." —GARRY SHANDLING

I have a friend who's so into recycling, she'll only marry a man who's been married before. —RITA RUDNER

I was best man at a wedding one time; that was pretty good. I thought it was a little too much in the title there. Best man. I think we ought to have the groom and a pretty good man. If I'm the best man, why is she marrying him? —JERRY SEINFELD

Every single one of my friends from high school has long since tied the knot. And I'm getting older; I guess I

should think about . . . hanging myself.
—LAURA KIGHTLINGER

> Men who have pierced ears are better
> prepared for marriage. They've
> experienced pain and bought jewelry.
> —RITA RUDNER

I went to a wedding. . . . I couldn't believe the groom was married in rented shoes. You're making a commitment for a lifetime, and your shoes have to be back by five-thirty. —JERRY SEINFELD

The two times they pronounce you anything in life is when you are man and wife or they pronounce you dead on arrival. —DENNIS MILLER

I married a younger man. Five years younger than I am. I figure it like this: If you can't find a good man, raise one. —WANDA SYKES-HALL

They say the secret to a successful marriage is leave. No, they say the secret is just don't go to bed angry. So I stayed awake for two years. —WENDY LIEBMAN

Most of the women in my family married for money, but not a lot of money. —LAURA KIGHTLINGER

On his wife: I was driving and I wanted to buy her freeway flowers at the off ramp. They were out of flowers. So I bought her a sack of oranges. She loves me. She put them in a vase. —BOB SAGET

My husband's Jewish—a nice Jewish boy. He'll never beat me. He won't tie me up like I want him to, but . . . —BRETT BUTLER

I love being married. It's so great to find that one special person you want to annoy for the rest of your life. —RITA RUDNER

I was married to a redneck from Macon, Georgia. Oh, I'm sorry; can you not say redneck anymore? Is that not politically correct? I will elaborate: I was married to a subliterate, terra-cotta–toothed imbecile with violent tendencies. Wait. Other words are coming to mind: I was married to a simian, knuckle-dragging, cousin-dating, nose-picking, trailor-dwelling, dog-selling, mother-loving, brainless amoeba, on the booger farm of the bayou. —BRETT BUTLER

On getting married: You lose the ability to get dressed by yourself. —PAUL REISER

All men make mistakes, but married men find out about them sooner. —RED SKELTON

I was so cold the other day, I almost got married. —SHELLEY WINTERS

Whatever you may look like, marry a man your own age. As your beauty fades, so will his eyesight. —PHYLLIS DILLER

On mixed marriages: You can tell the priest isn't into it 'cause he's saying things at the service like, "You know, I just think it's so great that these two people from different religions love each other so much that they don't mind going to hell." —JUDD APATOW

Now, of course, I realize that a mixed marriage means one between a man and a woman. —MICHAEL FELDMAN

After seven years of marriage, I'm sure of two things: First, never wallpaper together, and second, you'll need two bathrooms . . . both for her. The rest is a mystery, but a mystery I love to be involved in. —DENNIS MILLER

My wife still wants to talk in bed. We've been together seven years. I'm running out of things to say.
—DAMON WAYANS

They say marriage is a contract. No, it's not. Contracts come with warrantees. When something goes wrong, you can take it back to the manufacturer. If your husband starts acting up, you can't take him back to his mama's house. "I don't know; he just stopped working. He's just laying around making a funny noise."
—WANDA SYKES-HALL

I like a man that wears a wedding ring. 'Cause without it, they're like a shark without a fin. You pretty much got to know they're out there. —BRETT BUTLER

That's why I'm afraid of marriage. You have to make love to the same person for, like, three hundred years. How do you keep it exciting? Hats?
—ELAYNE BOOSLER

Basically my wife was immature. I'd be in my bath, and she'd come in and sink my boat. —WOODY ALLEN

It's a major adjustment for me to learn to live with another human being because I was raised by wolves.
—ELAYNE BOOSLER

He didn't have trouble committing . . . adultery. He was very unfaithful. He was cheating on me with his secretary. I'd find lipstick on his collar covered with Wite Out. —WENDY LIEBMAN

Eighty percent of married men cheat in America. The rest cheat in Europe. —JACKIE MASON

My cousin just got married for the totally wrong reasons. She married a man for money. She wasn't real subtle about it. Instead of calling him her fiancé, she kept calling him her financé. —RITA RUDNER

I highly recommend avoiding divorce at all costs. Well, maybe not all costs. Anything under $4 million.
—TOM ARNOLD

Divorce comes from the old Latin word *divorcerum,* meaning "having your genitals torn out through your wallet." —ROBIN WILLIAMS

I feel that my second marriage has finally prepared me for my first. —MICHAEL FELDMAN

Domestic Life

In my house, on the ceilings, I have paintings of the rooms above . . . so I never have to go upstairs.
—STEVEN WRIGHT

My house is filthy. Once a year, I wanna clean house, I call the cops. I go, "I've been robbed." They come over; they dust for fingerprints. Use your heads.
—JOAN RIVERS

It is the solemn duty of every landlord to maintain an adequate supply of roaches. The minimum acceptable roach-to-tenant ratio is four thousand to one.
—FRAN LEBOWITZ

My neighbor has a circular driveway. . . .
He can't get out.
—STEVEN WRIGHT

The problem with the designated driver program, it's not a desirable job. But if you ever get sucked into doing it, have fun with it. At the end of the night, drop them off at the wrong house. —JEFF FOXWORTHY

Sears Toughskins—reversible, polyester, ugly pants. Your knees will wear out before the pants do. —TIM ALLEN

I installed a skylight in my apartment. . . . The people who live above me are furious! —STEVEN WRIGHT

> Now, why does moisture ruin leather? Aren't cows outside a lot of the time? When it's raining, do cows go up to the farmhouse and say, "Let us in! We're wearing leather!"
> —JERRY SEINFELD

Have you noticed that if you leave the laundry in the hamper long enough, it's ready to wear again? —ELAYNE BOOSLER

Ever notice how irons have a setting for "permanent" press? I don't get it. . . . —STEVEN WRIGHT

This shirt is "dry-clean only." Which means it's dirty. —MITCH HEDBERG

Laundry's easier when you live alone. Fifteen minutes before a date, put 'em on, dry 'em with a hair blower. —ELAYNE BOOSLER

It doesn't matter what temperature a room is; it's always room temperature.
—STEVEN WRIGHT

I had my car stolen. Anybody ever had a car stolen from them? That is the worst feeling in the world because what happens is, you refuse to accept that it's your car is gone. I stood in the parking lot for two days; I was like, "Nah, they'll be back." —BILL BELLAMY

The way I see it, you've got friends, then you got your best friend. Big difference. To me, a friend is a guy who will help you move. A best friend is a guy who will help you move a body. —DAVE ATTELL

My house is made out of balsa wood, so when I want to scare the neighborhood kids, I lift it over my head and tell them to get out of my yard or I'll throw it at them. —STEVEN WRIGHT

It's very hard to sleep in your eye makeup and not wake up looking like Petie from the Little Rascals. —ELAYNE BOOSLER

Life is short. I don't care about the floor. I take vitamins; they drop; they roll under the refrigerator. I don't pick them up. I have five years of vitamins under the refrigerator. I'll probably come home one night and find a six-foot cockroach in Adidas saying, "I feel good!"
—ELAYNE BOOSLER

I moved into an all-electric house. I forgot and left the porch light on all day. When I got home, the front door wouldn't open. —STEVEN WRIGHT

The whole country is divorced, everybody lives by themselves, and they make bigger and bigger sizes of food. Does that make sense? Nobody thinks about us. Campbell's [is] the only company that even tried. Campbell's Soup for One. Seen it in the stores. Little teeny-tiny cans of Soup for One. Loneliest little can on the shelf; so much headroom on the shelf. Eight aisles away from the Party Mix, this stuff is. They try, but they really rub it in. Direction: Heat it up. Don't heat it up. Who gives a shit? You're alone. —ELAYNE BOOSLER

When you open a bag of cotton balls, is the top one meant to be thrown away?
—GEORGE CARLIN

The world is divided into good and bad people. The good ones sleep better . . . while the bad ones seem to enjoy the working hours much more. —WOODY ALLEN

Jews and blacks fighting each other. That has to be the dumbest thing I have ever heard of. What are we fighting about, who's got more people in show business? —JON STEWART

I'm not politically correct—I still say *black*. 'Cause *African American* doesn't give you no bonus. It doesn't make your life any easier. You don't see black people standing around saying, "Ohhh, yeah, African American, mmm-hmm-hmm; man, I tell you, this beats the hell out of being black. We should have made the switch years ago." —WANDA SYKES-HALL

Black crime tends to be stupid, not crazy. When you hear on the news that somebody chopped off his girlfriend's head, drank her blood, and used her toes to play pool, chances are, it was a white guy. Find an old lady kicked down the stairs for her welfare check. A black guy did it. —CHRIS ROCK

I wasn't always black. . . . There was this freckle, and it got bigger and bigger. —BILL COSBY

Rodney King has started his own record label. I think that's great, because if anyone can recognize a good beat, it's Rodney King. —CHRIS SPENCER

Now, personally, I am baffled by the concept of racial prejudice. Why hate someone based on the color of their skin when, if you take the time to get to know them as a human being, you can find so many other things to hate them for?
—DENNIS MILLER

Jews and blacks come from the same history. Two thousand years of bullshit, we've just expressed our suffering differently as people. Blacks developed the blues. Jews complain; we just never thought of putting it to music.
—JON STEWART

Do you realize there are now white people on *Soul Train* every week. Once upon a time, it was black people on *Soul Train,* white people on *American Bandstand.* Those were the rules! Attention, white people: Just because your s--t got canceled, don't come in and mess up our show, all right? —CHRIS ROCK

A group of white South Africans recently killed a black lawyer because he was black. That was wrong. They should have killed him because he was a lawyer.
—A. WHITNEY BROWN

According to census figures, whites are now officially a minority in Manhattan. And you know what? I am getting sick of being hassled by the man!
—DENNIS MILLER

I understand bigotry; I understand racism. My grandfather. Ninety years old, huge bigot. I love the man to death. Huge bigot. Hates immigrants. From Russia . . . hates immigrants. I guess my grandfather's one of those lucky immigrants who got off the boat, signed in, and then turned to the people behind him in line and went, "Now, get off my land!" —JON STEWART

Nabisco, the maker of the Oreo cookie, is announcing that they're cutting over three thousand jobs. It is all part of their new quota system where they'll have two black employees for every creamy-white employee.
—CONAN O'BRIEN

Black people have it bad. At least the Chinese and Italians have their own restaurants. . . . We don't even have our own food. —CHRIS ROCK

All Chinese names sound the same to me. I was in Chinatown one day and said, "Hey, you," and half the people turned around. They go, "Who me?" and the other half turned around. —GARRY SHANDLING

This country used to be owned by the red man, but he didn't give it up without a long, bloody fight. Don't you think it's time we colonists came down off our high horse and said, "We forgive you"? —DAVID CROSS AND BOB ODENKIRK

I had this dream that I was, like, driving down the freeway and slamming into everyone, just slamming into them. From side to side to side, right to left, all the way down the freeway. Not hurting any-one, though, just knocking the phones out of their hands.

—LAURA KIGHTLINGER

I no longer believe that it is right or proper for us to wear fur. I mean, it is summer, you know. . . .
—STEPHEN WRIGHT

In Kansas City, two homeless people who met at a soup kitchen were married in front of homeless guests at the very same soup kitchen. For those who want to give the couple a wedding gift, they're registered at Kansas City's District 5 Recycling Plant. —NORM MACDONALD

These paranoid people in the country that believe all these theories, they get on the Internet. You know, aliens landed in America and the government's keeping it a secret. Oh, yeah, because the government's **so** good at keeping secrets.
—JON STEWART

There are very few products that are environmentally pure, except some sneakers (Eco-Sneaks) and some safe, sustainable barbecue briquettes (Barbecue Fruit Wood Briquettes). Of course, if the sneakers come to you gift-wrapped, or if you actually use the briquettes to barbecue anything, the earth is again in peril.
—PAULA POUNDSTONE

In Arizona, Marine Corps engineers extended a steel barrier between the United States and Mexico by two and a half miles. It's all part of a plan to make illegal aliens walk an extra two and a half miles.
—NORM MACDONALD

I did a benefit for a feminist organization. All right, now you see, *benefit* means "no money," so I figure I can say whatever I want. And I figure if I pissed 'em off, who cares? What are they gonna do, get mad and pay me?
—WANDA SYKES-HALL

I got mugged. They got my knapsack with my comedy notebook in it. So if you see two **Cholos** bombing at the Funnybone chain, that would be them.

—JANEANE GAROFALO

I've never owned a gun. I won't allow one in the house. . . . Guns kept in the home for protection are forty-three times more likely to kill a family member than an assailant. Forty-three! "Hey, honey, I've brought something into the house that's forty-three times more likely to kill one of us than to do us any good." Maybe if the number was only thirty-three, I'd take my chances. —AL FRANKEN

I don't subscribe to a newspaper, but I just might so I can recycle and save a tree. —PAULA POUNDSTONE

Marrying a divorced man is ecologically responsible. In a world where there are more women than men, it pays to recycle. —RITA RUDNER

I grew up in a family where water conservation was a way of life. I still cringe when I see pictures of Niagara Falls. The whole thing looks to me like somebody is wasting a lot of good water. —LEWIS GRIZZARD

The filter's the best part. That's where they put the heroin. Only us real good smokers know that.
—DENIS LEARY

Here's what I don't understand about legalizing pot: Why? Why legalize it? Are you having trouble finding it? What? It's everywhere. Do you need it in the 7-Eleven 'cause you're too tired to walk to the park?
—JON STEWART

Crack is everywhere. People say it's destroying the black community. They say it's destroying the ghetto. Like the ghetto was so nice *before* crack? —CHRIS ROCK

Only in America would a guy invent crack. Only in America would there be a guy that cocaine wasn't good enough for. —DENIS LEARY

You know what I don't understand? How alcohol has escaped regulation in this country. That blows my mind. Here's how it is in this country: "Smoking will kill you. Drugs will ruin your life. Beer, it's magically delicious!" —JON STEWART

I would never do crack. I would never do a drug named after a part of my own ass.

—DENIS LEARY

All these animal rights people get on my nerves. They don't want to save all the animals, they just want to save the cute ones. You'll never see a "Save the Lab Rat" campaign. —DREW CAREY

Politicks

It's a popular delusion that the government wastes vast amounts of money through inefficiency and sloth. Enormous effort and elaborate plans are required to waste this much money. —P. J. O'ROURKE

According to a poll, 81 percent of the American public think the Bill of Rights is what you have to send in when you buy an appliance. —MICHAEL FELDMAN

What's right is what's left if you do everything else wrong. —ROBIN WILLIAMS

You watch politics on TV, man; there's more believable characters on *Melrose Place.* —JON STEWART

I can't believe the government has the nerve to limit the ways I can hurt myself. —DREW CAREY

Among black teenagers looking for jobs, nearly 40 percent can't find work. I can't understand why anyone would be against midnight basketball, which provides these guys with something to do and job training. Maybe the Republicans believe this is the kind of social welfare program that attracts undesirable immigrants. I do recall that a lot of the Haitian boat people mentioned they were looking forward to playing midnight basketball. —AL FRANKEN

The whole idea of our government is this: If enough people get together and act in concert, they can take something and not pay for it. —P. J. O'ROURKE

Anybody that wants drugs can get drugs. And the government's wasting all that money just pissing it away. Just so they can put on a big show for the people who are against drugs. Just 'cause those people happen to vote. —DREW CAREY

God saw everything he had made, and he saw that it was very good; and God said, "It just goes to show me what the private sector can accomplish. With a lot of fool regulations, this could have taken billions of years." —TONY HENDRA

Often, there are hardly any other senators in the chamber. Even the Senate avoids the Senate, because it's deadly dull in there.

—PAULA POUNDSTONE

I don't talk much about current events. I don't get the newspaper anymore, because my neighbor just moved. When I do buy the paper, I buy them out of the coin racks. They're cheaper. They're four for a quarter out of these things. —GARRY SHANDLING

What is a stealth bomber? It's a bomber that doesn't show up on radar, and you can't see it. Then we don't need one. —ROBIN WILLIAMS

Five thousand disabled Americans were in Washington, D.C., to protest doctor-assisted suicide. On a sad note, the demonstration turned ugly when all five thousand fought over two handicapped parking spaces.
—NORM MACDONALD

I didn't go to Washington for the Million Man March. I was actually there the next weekend for the thirty Jews pulling a falafel wagon. —JON STEWART

They want to put Reagan's head on Mount Rushmore. A couple of snags in the plan. They're not sure that granite is a dense enough material to accurately portray the former president's head. —DENNIS MILLER

Who among us will build that bridge to the twenty-first century? Who among us will fail to identify the correct cultural trends and end up living under that bridge?
—JON STEWART

Under a new law passed by the state assembly, effective next year, Michigan will set aside an allotment of hunting licenses for blind people. This after years of relentless lobbying by deer. —NORM MACDONALD

You must admit Louis Farrakhan is a very persuasive and charismatic leader. He has convinced thousands of people to wear bow ties, and that's not easy to do. —JON STEWART

A recent poll reported that most young people get the majority of their news from the late-night monologues of Letterman and Leno. Some have found this report disturbing. Of course, that's the reason such polls exist, to add to the disturbance level of the poll-reading classes. Surveys of young people perform an additional, essential function: They reinforce the perennial adult fear that the world is being handed over to a multitude of idiots who somehow lived in our homes for eighteen or twenty years. —HARRY SHEARER

I think we should take Iraq and Iran and combine them into one country and call it Irate. —DENIS LEARY

If all the nations in the world are in debt, where did the money go? —STEVEN WRIGHT

The mystery of government is not how Washington works but how to make it stop. —P. J. O'ROURKE

Democracy means that anyone can grow up to be president and anyone who doesn't grow up can be vice president.
—JOHNNY CARSON

Every politician we have, liberal or conservative, who gets caught drinking or chasing women is thrown out of office. It's backwards. It's more dangerous to have a clean-living president with his finger on the button. He thinks he's going right to heaven. You want to feel safe with a leader? Give me a guy who fights in bars and cheats on his wife. This is a man who wants to put off Judgment Day as long as possible. —LARRY MILLER

Anyone who is capable of getting themselves made president should on no account be allowed to do the job. —DOUGLAS ADAMS

President Clinton returned from a trip to the Balkans and announced that Bosnia is not Vietnam. Well, sure, just the fact that Clinton went there proves that.
—JAY LENO

A White House employee says President Clinton kissed and fondled her in an office at the White House and that it would have gone further but was interrupted by one of his illegal fund-raising calls. —BILL MAHER

I went to the inaugural balls. For $50,000 you could waltz with Hillary, for $25,000 you could tango with Tipper, and for just $25 you could get a lap dance from Janet Reno.
—AL FRANKEN

In Little Rock, two Arkansas state troopers testified that they helped then-governor Clinton cheat on his wife. You got three guys out looking for women, and the best you can come up with is Paula Jones? —JAY LENO

President Clinton spent the day on the phone with friends, who said that while he seemed upbeat, he didn't end his conversations with his trademark "Oh, God, yes!"
—CRAIG KILBORN

During a White House state dinner, a man's pants fell down while he was shaking hands with President Clinton. Which is rude, because proper etiquette says you should allow the president to drop his pants first.
—CONAN O'BRIEN

A child can go only so far in life without potty training. It is not mere coincidence that six of the last seven presidents were potty-trained, not to mention nearly half of the nation's state legislators. —DAVE BARRY

The Supreme Court has ruled that they cannot have a Nativity scene in Washington, D.C. This wasn't for any religious reasons. They couldn't find three wise men and a virgin. —JAY LENO

You have to remember one thing about the will of the people; last year, we were swept away by the Macarena.
—JON STEWART

Scientists said today that El Niño could cause huge food shortages on three continents. Sounds more like El Brando. —JAY LENO

I think China's getting kind of greedy. Now they want Britain to hand over the Spice Girls. —DAVID LETTERMAN

The Supreme Court ruled in favor of pornography on the Internet. Then, after the ruling, there was an awkward moment when Clarence Thomas started high-fiving everybody. —CONAN O'BRIEN

Scientists are comparing Mars' arid surface to Arizona—with one difference: The people of Mars willingly celebrate Martin Luther King Jr.'s birthday.
—CRAIG KILBORN

> Trickle down. The whole theory was this: We all have the money. If we drop some, it's yours. Go for it.
>   —BILL MAHER

An hour's perusal of our national charter makes it hard to understand what the argle-bargle is about. The First Amendment forbids infringements of the freedom of speech "except for commercials on children's television" or "unless somebody says '****' in a rap song or 'chick' on a college campus." The Second Amendment states that "the right of the people to keep and bear Arms, shall not be infringed," period. There is no mention of magazine size, rate of fire, or to what extent those arms may resemble assault rifles. —P. J. O'ROURKE

I think the reason justice is blind is because lawyers are jerking off all the time. —DENNIS MILLER

A secretary at a high school admitted to sleeping with four 17-year-old male students. As a result, she received thirty days in jail and four thank-you notes.
—CONAN O'BRIEN

The jury came in on the Oklahoma bombing trial. I guess they found him guilty. You could tell things weren't going well early on. Like, the jury sent out one note asking how many *e*'s there were in *electric chair*.
—JAY LENO

I hate people. People make me pronuclear.
—MARGARET SMITH

This country loves guns so much, we have a SaladShooter.

—BILL MAHER

It is said that life begins when the fetus can exist apart from its mother. By this definition, many people in Hollywood are legally dead. —JAY LENO

I think we ought to tear up all the freeways and give everything back to the Indians, just to see the look on their face. "Hey, sorry we screwed it up; good luck there, Chief Tumbling Dice." —TOM RHODES

Let's face it. America's one of the finest countries anyone ever stole. —BOBCAT GOLDTHWAIT

I mean, what is going on down at the post office? Every six months, some guy gets fired, comes back, and kills all his coworkers. If I worked at the post office as a supervisor, I wouldn't lay off anybody for the next twenty-five years. I'd just walk around saying, "Hanrohan, what are you doing?" "Nothing!" "Well, keep it up; you're doing a great job." —DENIS LEARY

The NRA scares me. If you own a gun, the odds of you actually protecting yourself are kinda slim. On the other hand, the odds of you getting liquored up and killing your mom over a meat loaf dispute are really high. —BOBCAT GOLDTHWAIT

Every election day, I have to hold my nose to vote.
—DREW CAREY

Giving money and power to government is like giving whiskey and car keys to teenage boys. —P. J. O'ROURKE

Now, the first thing they do when you join the armed forces is to strip you of any personal identity and make you indistinguishable from everybody around you. It's sort of like getting a sitcom on network television.
—DENNIS MILLER

If Newt Gingrich were cut in half, which end would grow back?
—MICHAEL FELDMAN

This country's only two hundred years old, and we've already had ten major wars. We average a major war every twenty years in this country, so we're good at it! And it's a good thing we are; we're not good at anything else anymore. Can't build a decent car, can't build a TV or a VCR . . . got no steel industry left, can't educate our children, can't give health care to our old people—but we can bomb the shit out of your country.
—GEORGE CARLIN

State legislators are merely politicians whose darkest secret prevents them from running for a higher office.
—DENNIS MILLER

See, when the GOVERNMENT spends money, it creates jobs; whereas when the money is left in the hands of TAXPAYERS, God only knows what they do with it. Bake it into pies, probably. Anything to avoid creating jobs. —DAVE BARRY

Last year, I had difficulty with my income tax. I tried to take my analyst off as a business deduction. The government said it was entertainment. Finally, we compromised, and made it a religious contribution. —WOODY ALLEN

Got a complaint about the Internal Revenue Service? Call the convenient toll-free-IRS-Taxpayer-Complaint-Hot-Line-number, 1-800-AUDITME. —DAVE BARRY

In reverse order, our last eight presidents: a hillbilly with a permanent hard-on; an upper-class bureaucrat-twit; an actor-imbecile; a born-again Christian peanut farmer; an unelected college football lineman; a paranoid moral dwarf; a vulgar cowboy criminal; and a mediocre playboy sex fiend. —GEORGE CARLIN

F-156 Peacekeeper missile. Doesn't that sound like Ax-murderer Baby-sitter?
—ELAYNE BOOSLER

I think if the postal service had any balls,
they would issue a series of stamps
commemorating all the people who have
been killed by mailmen.
—TOM KENNY

If at all possible, you should avoid being a young person
or a wheat farmer when the president starts feeling
international tension. —DAVE BARRY

A little government and a little luck are necessary in
life, but only a fool trusts either of them.
—P. J. O'ROURKE

Offensive Remarks on Religious Matters

In the beginning, there was nothing. God said, "Let there be light!" And there was light. There was still nothing, but you could see it a whole lot better.
—ELLEN DEGENERES

I love making fun of the Amish, know why? 'Cause they're never going to find out, that's why.
—DAVE ATTELL

If you still give money to Jimmy Swaggert, you deserve to be broke.
—BOBCAT GOLDTHWAIT

When faith is your guide, you better just stay on the bus. I know, because I got burned pretty bad on that Santa Claus story. I couldn't count all the nights I waited up for that fat geek to come down the chimney.
—A. WHITNEY BROWN

"Till death do you part." That's biblical times; Moses wrote that; that's in the Old Testament. That's way back then. See, they had no problem saying, "Till death do you part" back then. Because they didn't live that long. They had good plagues. Soon as that guy got on your nerves, here come some locusts to just come in to eat his ass up for you. —WANDA SYKES-HALL

I left the church when I was old enough. But they passed me on. They sent my address to the Jehovah's Witnesses. Five of them showed up one day and tried to gang-save me in my own living room. I never joined them, but I used to go to their church now and then. I liked it, because they always passed out plates of money at the end.

—A. WHITNEY BROWN

In Italy, Bob Dylan sang for Pope John Paul II and had a private audience with him. The pope said, "I speak eight different languages, and I still have no idea what he was saying." —CONAN O'BRIEN

I was raised by a religious cult, the Baptists. Their basic belief is that if you hold someone underwater long enough, he'll come around to your way of thinking. Bobbing for Baptists, they call it. —A. WHITNEY BROWN

Everybody loves the pope. The pope is the most loved man that nobody agrees with I've ever seen in my life. —JON STEWART

They taught me in Sunday school that the meek shall inherit the earth. I always hoped they would, because I was going to push them down and take it. I figured what could they do? A bunch of meeks. Even a wimp can whip a meek. —A. WHITNEY BROWN

The Big Guy

Apparently God went broke recently. All these TV evangelists raising money for God. Apparently God didn't put enough away when his kid had the carpentry business or something. —BOBCAT GOLDTHWAIT

It only rains straight down.
God doesn't do windows.
—STEVEN WRIGHT

I believe in God. I just think that maybe God's not watching out as closely for us as we might think. Look, he created the world in, what, six days, five billion years ago. Don't you think by now he's moved on to another project? Do you ever think we're something he just threw together for his third-grade science fair in the first place? —JON STEWART

Do you think God gets stoned? I think so. . . . Look at the platypus. —ROBIN WILLIAMS

I asked God what was in store for me today, like I do every morning. And he said, "Well, not so much that you couldn't turn your alarm off another five times." And I said, "Thank you, Lord; that's what I was thinking." —LAURA KIGHTLINGER

Suicide is our way of saying to God, "You can't fire me; I quit." —BILL MAHER

Who says life is sacred? God? Hey, if you read your history, God is one of the leading causes of death. —GEORGE CARLIN

Let's face it; God has a big ego problem. Why do we always have to worship him? —BILL MAHER

People of the Guilt

Religion shouldn't separate people. We all end up the same; we just get there in different ways. Jews are born with guilt. Catholics have to go learn it in school. —ELAYNE BOOSLER

I don't think Jews can be born again. A makeover, yes. . . .
—MICHAEL FELDMAN

You know who had faith? Jews had faith. They followed Moses through the desert for forty years. No map. There had to be one guy in the back saying, "Hey, I don't tink he knows vere he's goink. Forty years, vadda you kiddink me? I vas ten when vee started this trip!"
—ADAM FERRARA

You know what? I'm a Jewish guy; I've been to Israel. I'm really glad it's there, but I tell you what: There will never be peace there. Those are religious wars. Too many people have too many claims on too small a piece of land. Every major religion began in Israel; Christianity, Judaism, and Islam all began in Israel. All began in Jerusalem; all began within a two-block radius of each other. Jesus, Muhammad, and Moses all went to the same high school. —JON STEWART

I have a friend, actually, who wears a yarmulke that's knitted. He's so proud of it. "My girlfriend made it for me." Oh, that's great. Did you ever think that maybe she was making you a sweater and just thought f--k it?
—JON STEWART

In temple, I kept hearing Jewish men make good husbands. And I'm thinking, "Then who's this guy living in my house?" —BETSY SALKIND

I'm a Jewish guy. I can swear to you, there is no Jewish banking conspiracy. Do you know why? Jews can't agree with other Jews on where to go for dinner. There's no way we control the banks. We couldn't even get that meeting started. —JON STEWART

If Jesus was a Jew, how come he has a Mexican first name?

—BILLY CONNOLLY

Jewish people—we don't like to fight. Except in Israel, where we have Uzis. —ANDY KINDLER

Jewish people, we have a very simple philosophy in life: We just don't want to get rounded up again. That's an easy way to live your life—just walk down the street

avoiding trouble. "Ooh, someone's burning down the temple; I'll just go this way." Don't make a big deal out of it. Worship at a friend's house; nobody gets hurt.
—ANDY KINDLER

Cardinal O'Connor revealed he's coming out with an exorcise tape.
—MICHAEL FELDMAN

The Vatican is against surrogate mothers. Good thing they didn't have that rule when Jesus was born.
—ELAYNE BOOSLER

I went to an all-boys Catholic school. The name of it was Our Lady of the Sacred Pain in the Ass.
—JOHN LARROQUETTE

So what's the pope doing with body-guards and bulletproof glass? Is he afraid someone will shoot him? He'll die and he'll go to heaven? That would be horrible, huh? If the pope's afraid to die, what chance do we have?
—DREW CAREY

Police at Kennedy Airport arrested a Catholic priest with a gun. . . . The FDA estimates that for every priest with a gun they catch, forty nuns with rulers get through. —COLIN QUINN

I think we should all treat each other like Christians. I, however, will not be responsible for the consequences. —GEORGE CARLIN

Happy
Holidays

Do you know why, traditionally, we drink on New Year's Eve? Actually, it was done originally for health reasons. See, drinking the gin and scotch is nature's way of flushing the eggnog and fruitcake out of your system.

—JAY LENO

I did make some resolutions this year: to quit smoking, to exercise more, and to be kinder to my friends and small animals. And I kept those resolutions. For six whole days. And then I broke them. All of them. I feel bad about that, really bad. Not because I broke them, but because I wasted six whole days.

—A. WHITNEY BROWN

The only thing that bothers me more than dancing at a wedding is my mother dancing at a wedding.

—RAY ROMANO

You know, I hate the saying "Always a bridesmaid, never a bride." I like to put it into perspective by thinking, "Always a pallbearer, never a corpse."

—LAURA KIGHTLINGER

Every year when it's Chinese New Year in New York, there are fireworks going off at all hours. New York mothers calm their frightened children by telling them it's just gunfire. —DAVID LETTERMAN

Here's the holiday schedule for Monday's observation of Martin Luther King Jr.'s birthday, when the following will be closed: governmental offices, post offices, libraries, schools, banks, parts of Palm Beach, and the mind of Senator Jesse Helms of North Carolina.

—DENNIS MILLER

As a tip of his hat to Saint Patrick driving the snakes out of Ireland, Mayor Rudolph Giuliani and a contingent of New York's finest will use the parade to drive minorities out of Manhattan. —VANCE DEGENERES

The thing about painting yourself green is this: It's a great symbolic way to show your support of the Old Country and your family tree, but it's a terrible way to go out drinking. Mostly because your friends can't tell when you're about to puke. —DENIS LEARY

On the Saint Patrick's Day Parade: Later in the day, the revelers will wind their way through the streets of Manhattan, eventually ending up in northern Manhattan for the traditional beating of the Protestants.
—VANCE DEGENERES

Spring is Nature's way of saying,
"Let's party!"
—ROBIN WILLIAMS

I had a great Earth Day. I drove around with my muffler off, flicking butts out the window. Then I hit a deer. It's okay. I never hit a deer unless I intend to eat it.
—DREW CAREY

Earth Day was held recently. In honor of that event, I decided that I am just going to use only recycled jokes.
—DAVID LETTERMAN

It was the fifth of July, an easy day for an American to remember, because it's the day after ten days before Bastille Day. —A. WHITNEY BROWN

We have amazing holidays. Yom Kippur—Jewish day of atonement. You don't eat for one day. All your sins for the year are wiped clean. Beat that with your little Lent.

What is that? Forty days of absolution? Forty days to one. Even in sin you are paying retail. Wake up! Argue with the man. —JON STEWART

Let's say that Halloween is the devil's holiday, like he actually controls it and he's making a profit from it. What a lame-assed devil. You know, sitting down in the depths of hell saying, "Okay, let's see; I've got control of most of the major corporations on the planet. I've got them churning out toxic waste and weapons, and I'm controlling most of the media, too, and it's making people complacent and nonquestioning, and, my God, I've got thousands of millions of people who have sold their soul and given over their very integrity just for my will, but, but I need candy. —PATTON OSWALT

I know a lot of people have warm memories of their mothers' cooking, like Thanksgiving. I have no such memories. When I think of Thanksgiving, I have one memory: walking into the kitchen and seeing lots of pots of boiling water and plastic bags bobbing up and down. It was like Thanksgiving on the starship *Enterprise.* —FRANK MAYA

I still have my Christmas tree. I looked at it today. Sure enough, I couldn't see any forests. —STEVEN WRIGHT

On the 12th day of Christmas, my true love gave to me:
12-pack of Bud,
11 rasslin' tickets,
tin of Copenhagen,
9 years' probation,
8 table dancers,
7 packs of Red Man,
6 cans of SPAM,
5 flannel shirts,
4 big mud tires,
3 shotgun shells,
2 huntin' dawgs,
and some parts to a Mustang GT.
—JEFF FOXWORTHY

Holiday traditions mean a lot to people, particularly people in retail. . . . —MICHAEL FELDMAN

If you think *The Nutcracker* is something you did off the high-dive, you might be a redneck. —JEFF FOXWORTHY

Higher Learning

School Daze

I was coming home from kindergarten—well, they told me it was kindergarten. I found out later I had been working in a factory for ten years. It's good for a kid to know how to make gloves. —ELLEN DEGENERES

Having been unpopular in high school is not just cause for book publication. —FRAN LEBOWITZ

I often wonder if my perpetual sense of impending doom was caused by those *Dick and Jane* books we were forced to read as kids. What was Dick always running from? And why did he have to be told twice? Maybe I could have handled that sort of thing had I read it as an adult, but I suspect that reading *Dick and Jane* in our early childhood crippled many of us emotionally. —PAULA POUNDSTONE

In Wisconsin, a judge ruled that college students should have some say in how their tuition dollars are spent. Immediately after the ruling, the college kids decided to spend all their money on pot and Ramen noodles. —CONAN O'BRIEN

There are three things that school lunches have destroyed for twelve-year-olds: hot dogs, hamburgers, and pizza. You have to stay up pretty late to ruin pizza for a twelve-year-old. Even an English muffin with some Ragu and a slice of American cheese is better than the crap the schools give. —ADAM CORROLLA

I was thrown out of NYU my freshman year. I cheated on my metaphysics final in college. I looked within the soul of the boy sitting next to me. —WOODY ALLEN

I taught Sunday school for two years and I got fired. I abused my authority. I used to teach class like this: "Okay, if one more person talks, everybody is going to hell." I used to keep a list up on the board of who was going to burn.

—MARGARET CHO

Well, it's graduation time in high schools all over this country, and I'd like to take a moment to extend my sincere congratulations to that elite 49 percent of American students who made it through the system. You all worked very hard for your diplomas, and it's just too bad that more of you won't be able to read them.
—A. WHITNEY BROWN

On our educational system: Our kids have to pass through metal detectors simply to get an F minus in wood shop. —DENNIS MILLER

An article in *USA Today* says that bathroom graffiti in U.S. schools has reached an all-time high. The article also says, "For a good time, call Tracy." —CONAN O'BRIEN

I bought a self-learning record to learn Spanish. I turned it on and went to sleep; the record got stuck. The next day, I could only stutter in Spanish.

—STEVEN WRIGHT

I was terrible at history. I could never see the point of learning what people thought back when people were a lot stupider. For instance, the ancient Phoenicians believed that the sun was carried across the sky on the back of an enormous snake. So what? So they were idiots. —DAVE BARRY

You don't know what humiliation is until you've shown up for your first day of junior high in moon boots and a snowsuit that your mother got on sale during the summer. I looked like a demented astronaut. —DREW CAREY

Deep. Very Deep.

Original thought is like original sin; both happened before you were born to people you could not possibly have met. —FRAN LEBOWITZ

The proof that we don't understand death is we give dead people a pillow. I mean, if you can't stretch out and get some solid rest at that point, I don't think there are any bedding accessories that can make the difference. —JERRY SEINFELD

If you know the average person is stupid, then realize half are stupider than that.
—GEORGE CARLIN

A common mistake that people make when trying to design something completely foolproof is to underestimate the ingenuity of complete fools.
—DOUGLAS ADAMS

Why are some places wealthy and other places poor? It occurred to me, at least, that this might have something to do with money. —P. J. O'ROURKE

My definition of an intellectual is someone who can listen to the *William Tell* Overture without thinking of the Lone Ranger. —BILLY CONNOLLY

You must remember that then, as now, it remained the single most important function of a generation to irk the living shit out of the generation immediately preceding it. —DENNIS MILLER

I've got this real moron thing I do; it's called thinking. —GEORGE CARLIN

Sometimes something worth doing is worth overdoing. —DAVID LETTERMAN

Of course, it's very easy to be witty tomorrow, after you get a chance to do some research and rehearse your ad libs. —JOEY ADAMS

I refuse to answer that question on the grounds that I don't know the answer. —DOUGLAS ADAMS

Perhaps the good life's secret lies in civilization. The Chinese had an ancient and sophisticated civilization when my relatives were hunkering naked in trees. (Admittedly, that was last week, but they'd been drinking.) —P. J. O'ROURKE

Everyone is entitled to an individual opinion. It just happens that yours is wrong. —DAVE BARRY

I got a lot of ideas. Trouble is, most of them suck.
—GEORGE CARLIN

There's a difference between information and knowledge. It's the difference between Christy Turlington's phone number and Christy Turlington. —P. J. O'ROURKE

Life is anything that dies when you stomp on it.
—DAVE BARRY

Life is full of loneliness, misery, and suffering, and it's all over much too soon. —WOODY ALLEN

I think there's life in outer space, sure. But they think we're the Alabama of the universe. They know we're here; they just want nothing to do with us.
—TOM RHODES

The only thing that scares me more than space aliens is the idea that there aren't any space aliens. We can't be the best that creation has to offer. I pray we're not all there is. If so, we're in big trouble.
—ELLEN DEGENERES

A penny saved is worthless. —DAVE BARRY

I think the cliché is true that money doesn't buy happiness. . . . It can actually let you focus more time on your misery. —GARRY SHANDLING

It's a small world, but I wouldn't want to have to paint it. —STEVEN WRIGHT

> In the beginning, the universe was created. This has made a lot of people very angry and been widely regarded as a bad move.
> —DOUGLAS ADAMS

Never look where you're going; you'll only scare yourself. —P. J. O'ROURKE

What does not kill me makes me funnier.
—DENNIS MILLER

I argue very well. Ask any of my remaining friends. I can win an argument on any topic, against any opponent. People know this, and steer clear of me at parties. Often, as a sign of their great respect, they don't even invite me. —DAVE BARRY

He felt that his whole life was some kind of dream, and he sometimes wondered whose it was and whether they were enjoying it. —DOUGLAS ADAMS

I don't know what makes people violent. Some experts say television. I'm sure it does. But I know that the Nazis didn't watch a lot of TV, and something tells me the Serbs weren't watching a lot of *The A-Team* during the seventies. —AL FRANKEN

Always keep your anger bottled up. You might need a bottle of anger someday when friends come by and don't leave. —LAURA KIGHTLINGER

You will never find anybody who can give you a clear and compelling reason why we observe "daylight saving time."
—DAVE BARRY

I have tended to view my acts of conservation as some sort of retirement-account deposit. As if, when the earth appears drained of every last bit of fossil fuel, there will be a few more full gas tanks set aside for me because of the time I walked to my therapist instead of driving.
—PAULA POUNDSTONE

You can never trust what you read. Which is why I never read. Thank God I never learned to read; now I'm never misled. —ADAM CORROLLA

Human beings, who are almost unique in having the ability to learn from the experience of others, are also remarkable for their apparent disinclination to do so. —DOUGLAS ADAMS

Kulture

How many people watch X-rated movies? Two. I don't even know why they make them. They must be losing a fortune on those things. —RICHARD JENI

I only buy **Hustler** 'cause I like to hide the **Post** in something on the way home.
—ELAYNE BOOSLER

My favorite *Star Trek* incarnation? *The Next Generation.* Because of Jean-Luc Picard. Who knew? Who knew a short bald man could be so hot? —SUE MURPHY

I'm on the road for, like, sixteen weeks at a time, going, "Gee, I never noticed it before, but Judy Jetson doesn't have a bad ass. She's attractive in a futuristic sort of way." —RICHARD JENI

. . . I got a CD of traditional Indian music, from India. Go ahead and laugh, but there's a song on there fifty-nine minutes long. That's value. I'm telling you it's twenty minutes before the drums kick in, but if you're really listening, they couldn't come in a second sooner. —MARC MARON

You know why I like doing comedy the most? Because when I'm performing, I look out on the audience and I look at all these people and my ego goes, "All these people came to see you tonight!" And then I remember that mechanical bulls used to be real popular, too. —BOBCAT GOLDTHWAIT

I take music pretty seriously. See that scar on my wrist? You see that? Know what it's from? I heard the Bee Gees were getting back together again, and I couldn't take it.

—DENIS LEARY

Do you think that Beethoven ever did a bad song? He was such a genius. Did Beethoven ever sit down at the piano and go, "Everybody was Kung Fu fighting"?
—ARSENIO HALL

Let me make sure I am crystal clear on this issue, okay? Heavy metal fans are buying heavy metal records, taking the records home, listening to the records, and then blowing their heads off with shotguns. Where's the problem? —DENIS LEARY

We can't re-create the sixties, not even if we wanted to. We just don't have what it takes these days. There aren't enough politicians left worth killing.
—P. J. O'ROURKE

My favorite toy . . . Crayola sixty-four box. It's like a child's orgasm. —CATHY LADMAN

Be honest; how many times have you gone to a multi-screen theater complex and just stood there, looking up at the marquee, trying to decide which movie sucked the least? —DENNIS MILLER

In recent years, Oscars have gone to pictures where someone was either dying horribly starving in a cave, dying horribly freezing in the North Atlantic, or dying

horribly getting drawn and quartered in twelfth-century Scotland. (How do you keep that theme and make it relevant to today? A film about dying horribly being crushed by a shipment of relaxed-fit jeans at the Gap?)
—TONY KORNHEISER

An ambitious and aggressive mother conned pianist Arthur Rubinstein into listening to her ten-year-old son murder a nocturne by Chopin. At the conclusion of the massacre, Rubinstein announced, "Madam, that is undoubtedly the worst piano playing I ever heard." Whereupon the mother nodded happily and told her son, "You see, stupid? Now will you give up those expensive piano lessons and try out for the Little League baseball team?" —ART BUCHWALD

On salsa dancing: I thought I was doing really well, and then I overheard the evil woman in the corner saying, "Oh, look at the deaf girl trying." —CAROLINE RHEA

After a few boring years, socially meaningful rock 'n' roll died out. It was replaced by disco, which offers no guidance to any form of life more advanced than the lichen family. —DAVE BARRY

CBS canceled twelve shows. This network has tested more bombs than India. —DAVID LETTERMAN

Listen, bad television is three things: a bullet train to a morally bankrupt youth; a slow spiral into an intellectual void; and, of course, a complete blast to watch.
—DENNIS MILLER

Everyone has a purpose in life. Perhaps yours is watching television. —DAVID LETTERMAN

Here's the problem with TV. All people on TV are TV people, and TV people are dumber than the dumbest guys you went to high school with—they just dress better. —ADAM CORROLLA

The real trouble started when we got the contestants mixed up for the dumb human tricks and the stupid pet tricks. They look so much alike. —DAVID LETTERMAN

Life doesn't imitate art, it imitates bad television.
—WOODY ALLEN

Imitation is the sincerest form of television.
—FRED ALLEN

I love the music of the eighties. It was such an "Oh, Micky, you're so fine" time. —MARGARET CHO

If you surveyed a hundred typical middle-aged Americans, I bet you'd find that only two of them could tell you their blood types, but every last one of them would know the theme song from *The Beverly Hillbillies*.
—DAVE BARRY

In Springfield, Missouri, the local cable company mistakenly aired five minutes of explicit sex scenes from the Playboy Channel on the Cartoon Network, during an episode of *The Flintstones*. Children who saw the broadcast called it the greatest *Flintstones* episode ever.
—NORM MACDONALD

I was obsessed with Saturday morning cartoons, which I still love, but then it was always so sad because you knew it was all over when *Soul Train* came on.
—MARGARET CHO

The sixties were when hallucinogenic drugs were really, really big. And I don't think it's a coincidence that we had the type of shows we had then, like *The Flying Nun*.
—ELLEN DEGENERES

Working Stiffs

Engineering majors—we don't get laid much, but we're building the future. —ROBIN WILLIAMS

I thought about forming a support group for workavoidics, but it doesn't seem worth the effort. —MICHAEL FELDMAN

I find it rather easy to portray a businessman. Being bland, rather cruel, and incompetent comes naturally to me. —JOHN CLEESE

If you want to get ahead in this world, get a lawyer, not a book.
—FRAN LEBOWITZ

I got a chain letter by fax. It's very simple. You just fax a dollar bill to everybody on the list. —STEVEN WRIGHT

I was watching this documentary on a woman who pulled every hair out of her head. I just admire anyone who can finish what they start. —LAURA KIGHTLINGER

Shakespeare said, "Kill all the lawyers." There were no agents then. —ROBIN WILLIAMS

Most people don't realize how many jobs are created by one porno film. Of course, we immediately think of the actresses and actors. But what about the technicians who do the lighting and sound? Porno films provide many of the crucial entry-level jobs that are so important to expanding our workforce. —AL FRANKEN

H. J. Heinz has announced plans to lay off three thousand workers. According to company spokesmen, employees who refuse to budge will be turned over and shaken vigorously until they slide out.
—NORM MACDONALD

So before I did stand-up, I was a secretary. And like a lot of secretaries, I practically ran that company. Into the ground. —WENDY LIEBMAN

I think crime pays. The hours are good; you travel a lot.
—WOODY ALLEN

Whether you're going off to college or straight to prison, remember: There will always be a long line of harder working, less demanding immigrants ready to take your job if you start slacking off.
—A. WHITNEY BROWN

I used to work at an inconvenience store. We had no shelves. Everything was just in a big pile. We had no change. "I can't break that one. Sit over there; it's gonna be a couple of hours. Hey, this is an inconvenience store; you're lucky I'm even talking to you; that's against store policy. Usually I just stand around and give everyone the finger." —ROB SCHNEIDER

I had the meanest boss in the world, so I would call in sick a lot. I'd call her up and say, "female problems." She didn't know I meant her. —WENDY LIEBMAN

If you had to identify in one word the reason why the human race has not achieved, and never will achieve, its full potential, that word would be *meetings*. —DAVE BARRY

I don't know what it's like to drive a cab. It must be very difficult, because they're very upset, these people. And sometimes you just want to lean over the seat and go, "What is happening in your life and your mind that is making you drive like this? Take it easy." —JERRY SEINFELD

I had the most boring office job in the world. I used to clean the windows on envelopes. —RITA RUDNER

If God wanted us to bend over, he'd put diamonds on the floor. —JOAN RIVERS

No drug, not even alcohol, causes the fundamental ills of society. If we're looking for the sources of our troubles, we shouldn't test people for drugs, we should test them for stupidity, ignorance, greed, and love of power. —P. J. O'ROURKE

You know how I describe the economic and social classes of this country? The upper class keeps all of the money, pays none of the taxes. The middle class pays all of the taxes, does all of the work. The poor are there to scare the shit out of the middle class. Keep 'em showing up at those jobs. —GEORGE CARLIN

> You know you're never more indignant in life than when you're shopping in a store that you feel is beneath you and one of the other customers mistakes you for an employee of that store.
> —DENNIS MILLER

I went to a garage sale. "How much for the garage?" "It's not for sale." —STEVEN WRIGHT

People are still willing to do an honest day's work. The trouble is, they want a week's pay for it. —JOEY ADAMS

Does anybody believe your health is more important than money? I don't see too many beautiful women saying, "Hey, should I sleep with Bill in the Porsche or Dave with low cholesterol?" —NICK DIPAOLO

Money is better than poverty, if only for financial reasons. —WOODY ALLEN

The only thing money gives you is the freedom of not worrying about money. —JOHNNY CARSON

Money doesn't talk, it swears. —BOB DYLAN

Bankruptcy is a legal proceeding in which you put your money in your pants pocket and give your coat to your creditors. —JOEY ADAMS

I had a nest egg, but I lost it gambling. . . . I was betting I'd be dead by now. —DREW CAREY

A genius is one who can do anything except make a living. —JOEY ADAMS

I lost my job. No, not really. I know where my job is. It's just that when I go there, a new guy is doing it.
—BOBCAT GOLDTHWAIT

There's no business like show business, but there are several businesses like accounting. —DAVID LETTERMAN

In medical news, there are reports that suicide doctor Jack Kevorkian isconsidering retirement. As Kevorkian put it: "I always said I'd quit the day it stopped being fun." —NORM MACDONALD

The easiest job in the world has to be coroner. You perform surgery on dead people. What's the worst thing that can happen? If everything went wrong, maybe you'd get a pulse. —DENNIS MILLER

For
Recreational
Use Only

Around the House

There are two kinds of home-repair projects: those too big to undertake yourself and those too small to bother with. The first kind, you can't afford, and the second kind, if left alone, will develop into something you can't afford either. —P. J. O'ROURKE

> There is a very fine line between "hobby" and "mental illness."
> —DAVE BARRY

In my house, there's this light switch that doesn't do anything. Every so often, I would flick it on and off just to check. Yesterday, I got a call from a woman in Madagascar. She said, "Cut it out." —STEVEN WRIGHT

Women—they don't understand a man's propensity for building useless shit. I'm in there fashioning a bird feeder one day, and I realize to myself, "You know, I don't really like birds all that much." So I customized it and made it a combination bird feeder—cat feeder. —TIM ALLEN

Basically, a tool is an object that enables you to take advantage of the laws of physics and mechanics in such a way that you can seriously injure yourself.
—DAVE BARRY

Animal House

My dog watches me on TV. So, if I may take this opportunity: "No! No! No!" —GARRY SHANDLING

I had a dog. He was a good dog. Of course, back then, a good dog was still just a good dog. These days, I suppose, he'd be a Canine American.
—A. WHITNEY BROWN

The FDA approved a Prozac-type drug for dogs who are depressed. Which is good, because it's hard for dogs to get therapy, since they're never allowed on the couch. —COLIN QUINN

Dogs who earn their living by appearing on television commercials in which they constantly and aggressively demand meat should remember that in at least one Far Eastern country, they *are* meat. —FRAN LEBOWITZ

We take pets too seriously in this country. We don't even have doggy kennels anymore, we have doggy hotels. We've got people sleeping on the streets in this country, yet somewhere there's a poodle pissed off because a maid didn't leave a liver snap on his pillow last night. —NICK DIPAOLO

I have no idea what dogs get out of hunting. And once I started to think about that, I realized I didn't have much of an idea what people get out of hunting either.
—P. J. O'ROURKE

On my way to work this week, I drove by a sign that read: DOG DAY CARE. And I thought, "That's God's way of saying there are folks who make much too much money. Day care for dogs. What will they think of next, gestalt for gerbils?" —TONY KORNHEISER

Dogs would make totally incompetent criminals. If you could somehow get a group of dogs to understand the concept of the Kennedy assassination, they would all immediately confess to it. Whereas you'll never see a cat display any kind of guilty behavior, despite the fact that several cats were seen in Dallas on the grassy knoll area, not that I wish to start rumors. —DAVE BARRY

If only someone would do for cows what Bambi did for deer. Cows have been in films, but they haven't starred. I'm still willing to eat a species that is only a supporting player. —PAULA POUNDSTONE

I was in the grocery store. I saw a sign that said: PET SUPPLIES. So I did. Then I went outside and saw a sign that said: COMPACT CARS. —STEVEN WRIGHT

My cat was up all night throwing up. So obviously I was up all night holding her hair.
—SARAH SILVERMAN

After blowing marijuana smoke into your cat's mouth, make sure that there is plenty of accessible string nearby. —DENNIS MILLER

Officials at the Bronx Zoo say they are not worried about a male gorilla who refuses to mate with the female gorillas. However, the officials admit they are a little concerned that he likes to dress up like Liza Minnelli. —CONAN O'BRIEN

Young man on acid, thought he could fly, jumped out of a building. What a tragedy. If he thought he could fly,

why didn't he take off from the ground first? You don't see ducks lining up to catch elevators to fly south.
—BILL HICKS

The other day when I was walking through the woods, I saw a rabbit standing in front of a candle making shadows of people on a tree. —STEVEN WRIGHT

I was reading something about *Penthouse* Pet of the Year the other day. That's a dubious title, isn't it? Pet of the Year. What do you have to do to get that, go on the paper? —ELAYNE BOOSLER

Cockroaches have been given a bad rap. They don't bite, smell, or get into your booze. —P. J. O'ROURKE

Weird World of Sports

Men forget everything; women remember everything. That's why men need instant replays in sports. They've already forgotten what happened. —RITA RUDNER

My boyfriend is shorter than I am, and we were talking about sports, and just out of the blue, I said, "When you

were in grade school, did you play midget football?" He got really mad and said, "What?" and I said, "Well, it's not like I said, 'Did you play football, midget?'"
—LAURA KIGHTLINGER

I was watching the Super Bowl with my ninety-two-year-old grandfather. The team scored a touchdown. They showed the instant replay. He thought they scored another one. I was gonna tell him, but I figured the game he was watching was better. —STEVEN WRIGHT

In a recent interview, Dennis Rodman said the NBA can kiss his ass. Then later, he asked the NFL to fondle his nipples.
—CONAN O'BRIEN

Karate is a form of martial arts in which people who have had years and years of training can, using only their hands and feet, make some of the worst movies in the history of the world. —DAVE BARRY

It is so tough being a sports fan in Cleveland sometimes. Summertime's the worst 'cause everybody makes fun of the Indians. 'Cause, you know, they kinda suck. I know they try hard and everything, but it doesn't matter 'cause they suck. That's not even the worst part: They know they suck. You know they suck. And they know you know they suck. —DREW CAREY

Men hate to lose. I once beat my husband at tennis. I asked him, "Are we going to have sex again?" He said, "Yes, but not with each other." —RITA RUDNER

I remember summer mornings, slipping out the back door, barefoot, with a straw hat on my head and a cane pole slung over my shoulder. I always felt like an idiot on the bus in that getup, though. —A. WHITNEY BROWN

Although golf was originally restricted to wealthy, over-weight Protestants, today it's open to anybody who owns hideous clothing. —DAVE BARRY

NikeTown Los Angeles has display racks full of shoes specifically for hiking, climbing, golf, basketball, running, volleyball, skateboarding, soccer, and wrestling. I didn't buy any because they didn't have a pair specifically designed for my sport, which is sitting.
—PAULA POUNDSTONE

I was captain of the latent-paranoid softball team. . . . I used to steal second base, and feel guilty and go back.
—WOODY ALLEN

An avid skier I know has the bumper sticker PRAY FOR
NUCLEAR WINTER. —MICHAEL FELDMAN

Skiing combines outdoor fun with knocking down trees
with your face. —DAVE BARRY

There's a fine line between fishing and standing on the
shore looking like an idiot. —STEVEN WRIGHT

I go fishing. One of these professional fisherman tells
me to go to the end of the lake, where the fish are
spawning. . . . I don't want to bother them when they're
doing that. I don't want to be making love and have
someone dangle pizza over the bed.
—GARRY SHANDLING

I stayed up all night playing poker
with tarot cards. I got a full house
and four people died.
—STEVEN WRIGHT

A baseball player who makes a spectacular defensive
play always leads off the next inning as batter.
—BOB SMITH

The last professional hockey player to play without a helmet announced he's retiring. His actual words were, "I no play hockey never more." —CONAN O'BRIEN

Funky Fashions

I don't wear bikini underwear. You know why? Because I am considerate of my fellow human beings.
—DREW CAREY

This is actually an old tie. It's from the fifties. It doesn't look really out of place in this era. You know, I think everything comes back around again. Except for powdered wigs for men. That will never make the full circle, I don't think.

—ERIC TUNNEY

Always remember that if editors were so damned smart, they would know how to dress. —DAVE BARRY

People have been obsessed with fashion
ever since the Garden of Eden,
when Eve said to Adam, "You know, that
fig leaf you have on is so last-season."
—DENNIS MILLER

High heels should be outlawed (at the very least, there should be a five-day waiting period before you can buy them). They destroy your feet. It should be mandatory that the surgeon general print a warning label on high heels like they do a package of cigarettes (i.e., "Warning: These shoes can lead to lower-back pain, aching toes, and the illusion that you're taller than you actually are."). —ELLEN DEGENERES

I wear ties only to funerals of close relatives or heads of state. I'm convinced ties restrict the blood flow to the brain, causing such disorders as forgetfulness, blurred eyesight, and even criminal tendencies. (Al Capone was rarely seen without a tie. The same goes, incidentally, for Richard Nixon.) —LEWIS GRIZZARD

The idea behind the tuxedo is the woman's point of view that "men are all the same, so we might as well dress them that way." That's why a wedding is like the joining together of a beautiful, glowing bride and some

guy. The tuxedo is a wedding safety device, created by women because they know men are undependable. So in case the groom chickens out, everybody just takes one step over, and she marries the next guy.
—JERRY SEINFELD

I hate fashion. . . . They have these runway shows, and they have a commentator saying, "A pretty face is your best asset this season." As opposed to last season, when ugly girls had a free ride all the way through. When back-fat was all the rage. —JANEANE GAROFALO

I think high heels are ridiculous. It's like putting a building on the head of a pin. —CATHY LADMAN

Hitler has pretty much put the kibosh on that mustache style. Have you noticed that there is nobody but nobody wearing the Hitler mustache? That guy ruined it for everybody. What a jerk he was. —ERIC TUNNEY

A Cavalcade of Stars

I went to see a slasher movie last night. It was good, but the guy in back of me ruined the film. This guy is going, "Oh, that's not real! That's not how you do it! Gimme a break! You don't hold the knife that way!" I turned around and said, "Look, O. J., will you shut up, please?"
—JAY LENO

Oprah Winfrey issued a statement saying that even though she appeared on the *Ellen* coming-out episode, she's not gay. Meanwhile, Ellen DeGeneres issued a statement saying even though she appeared on *Oprah,* she's not black. —CONAN O'BRIEN

I had this woman come up to me and say, "I don't want to insult you, but you look like Bobcat Goldthwait."
—BOBCAT GOLDTHWAIT

That's what's wrong in this country; we always shoot the wrong guys. We shoot JFK; we shoot RFK. It comes to Teddy, we say, "Aw, leave him alone. . . ."
—DENIS LEARY

The other day, Congressman Joe Kennedy and his son had a minor mishap with some illegal fireworks. When asked about it, Kennedy said, "We're trying to find alternatives to alcohol and underage women."
—CONAN O'BRIEN

Ted Kennedy—a good senator, but a bad date.
—DENIS LEARY

At the Gap, they have a special changing cubicle just for celebrities—it's just like all the others, except it has a star on the door and a bowl of fruit inside. Also, you're not limited to three items, you can bring in four.
—ELLEN DEGENERES

I have a little crick in my neck tonight from watching Hasselhoff hold in his stomach on **Baywatch**.
—DENNIS MILLER

Today is David Hasselhoff's birthday. He said his birthday wish is that the world continues its juvenile obsession with giant breasts. —CONAN O'BRIEN

You know how you can tell if you're Jewish. If you're watching the Pamela Anderson Lee video and you think, "Nice boat!" —GARY SHANDLING

Pamela Lee had an all-natural birth at her Malibu home. Only in L.A. do you have bleached hair, silicone breasts, and an all-natural birth. —JAY LENO

Anna Nicole Smith's boyfriend is being charged with smuggling heroin. Prosecutors say he'll be in prison so long that when he gets out, she'll be really interested in him. —CONAN O'BRIEN

I think Superman should go on the *Larry King* show and announce that he would come back to life if people in all fifty states wanted him to. —DAVE BARRY

She has a very sharp wit, and she wields it like a blunt instrument.

—STONE PHILLIPS

If Ricky Schroder and Gary Coleman had a fight on television with pool cues, who would win? (1) Ricky Schroder (2) Gary Coleman (3) the television-viewing public? —DAVID LETTERMAN

I find it hard to believe that Elvis Presley faked his death. 'Cause he died on the can. I mean, if I was going to fake my death, I wouldn't be pounding one out. —BOBCAT GOLDTHWAIT

I feel sorry for Elvis Presley, how his family buried him in the backyard. Guess they didn't call him King for nothing. —DREW CAREY

Michael Jackson is the polar opposite of President Clinton if you think about it. In many respects, Michael Jackson and President Clinton are diametrically opposite. Michael Jackson is constantly, constantly, desperately trying to make us believe he's having sex with women.
—DAVID LETTERMAN

The other day, fifteen Boy Scouts from Minnesota had to be rescued after they became lost in the Cascade mountains. At first, rescuers tried to find the boys with bloodhounds, and when that didn't work, they brought in Michael Jackson. —CONAN O'BRIEN

We live in a country where John Lennon takes six bullets in the chest and Yoko Ono is standing right next to him and not one bullet. Explain it to me.

—DENIS LEARY

Calista Flockhart will appear on the big screen this year. She'll play an underweight woman who's locked in a cage and force-fed mass quantities of high-fat dairy products. It's called *Ally McVeal*. —RICHARD BELZER

Mickey Mouse to a three-year-old is a six-foot-tall RAT!
—ROBIN WILLIAMS

Every year at Rockefeller Plaza, they have the big Christmas tree there above the ice-skating rink . . . and it came from upstate. And this year, for the first time, they cut down the tree, seventy-four-foot Christmas tree, and they delivered it—put it on a barge and sailed it down the Hudson to get here. And I was thinking, coincidentally, maybe you know this, that's how Rush Limbaugh gets to work every day. —DAVID LETTERMAN

Richard Lewis. Jon Stewart. Four first names. What are we hiding from? —JON STEWART

According to researchers in Australia, koala bears have fingerprints so close to those of humans, they could easily be mistaken by police at the scene of a crime. It should be noted, however, the research was funded by O. J. Simpson. —NORM MACDONALD

You know who used to scare me? That crazy cult leader from Texas, um, uh . . . Perot. —JON STEWART

Madonna and I are close friends. But we're very different. She sleeps with her trainer; I ignore mine.

—ROSIE O'DONNELL

I find it hard to believe that John Lennon had a sneaker commercial in mind when he wrote "Revolution."
—BOBCAT GOLDTHWAIT

I was reading an interview with Keith Richards recently in a magazine, and in the interview, Keith Richards intimated that kids should not do drugs. . . . Keith, we can't do any more drugs, because you already did them all! There's none left; we have to wait until you die and smoke your ashes! —DENIS LEARY

Asked by reporters about his upcoming marriage to a forty-two-year-old woman, director Roman Polanski told reporters, "The way I look at it, she's the equivalent of three 14-year-olds." —DAVID LETTERMAN

For horror fans, Wes Craven will produce and direct *Martha Stewart: Living Dead*. Martha Stewart will be played by a look-alike she makes herself from some compost, potpourri, and homegrown basil.
—RICHARD BELZER

Sat next to Daniel Day-Lewis on the plane out. He says he's trying to lose 137 pounds in order to play a newborn baby in Scorsese's next project. —DENIS LEARY

Sam Donaldson once said on *David Brinkley* that a sketch I wrote "just wasn't funny." I'll tell you what, Sam. You don't make rules about comedy; I won't make rules about hair. —AL FRANKEN

Steven Spielberg has signed a deal to produce a new show for CBS. Apparently, he's going to utilize the same technology he used in *Jurassic Park* to animate the cast of *60 Minutes.* —CONAN O'BRIEN

You know what they say when a supermodel gets pregnant: "Now she's gonna be eating for one." —JAY LENO

I went down to the Fashion Cafe to get into the celebration of Fashion Week and made a terrible mistake. . . . I hung up my coat on Kate Moss. —DAVID LETTERMAN

John Gotti underwent surgery. Doctors removed a cancerous tumor near his tonsils. Then they took the tumor, drove it to New Jersey, and shot it in the head ten times. —CHRIS ROCK

The one good thing about living out there is you see a lot of celebrities. I'm kinda starstruck still, in L.A. I saw Sally Struthers on the street the other day, that was kinda cool. Gave her a dollar. . . . Felt bad for her. —DREW CAREY

I have a theory about Tonya Harding: It's not her fault what happened to her. Anybody named Tonya is not expected to amount to anything. —BRETT BUTLER

Bill Gates paid $30 million for a Winslow Homer painting of a seascape. However, he will continue to pay four bucks for a haircut. —COLIN QUINN

Jesse Jackson said it pains him that when he's walking down the street at night and hears footsteps, he's relieved if it's a white man and not a black man. I know exactly what he means. I was leaving NBC late one night and heard some footsteps. When I turned around, I saw it was Jesse Jackson, and it scared the living daylights out of me! —AL FRANKEN

Next month, the U.S. Postal Service will begin issuing stamps depicting Dracula, the Mummy, and Frankenstein's monster. The stamps are part of a new series called "People Who Abbott and Costello Have Met." —NORM MACDONALD

Saw Adam West on CNN not long ago, whining that he didn't get to play Batman in the movie. Now, here's a guy with a stranglehold on reality, huh? That's the first thing I look for in a superhero, a distended belly. —DENNIS MILLER

Hosting the Academy Awards is like being married to Larry King. You know that it's going to be painful, but it will also be over in about three hours.

—DAVID LETTERMAN

I think we're making a step forward, because now rock stars are dying in treatment centers instead of hotel rooms. —GEORGE CARLIN

David Helfgott said playing for the Academy audience reminded him of playing at the mental hospital. Half the people were on medication and half had delusions of grandeur. —BILL MAHER

In honor of Frank Sinatra's birthday, the Empire State Building is covered in blue light. . . . And, of course, the observation tower is covered with a giant toupee.
—DAVID LETTERMAN

A new study shows that one out of every four drivers has fallen asleep at the wheel while on the road. And for half of those, the last thing they remember hearing is: "And now, here's a new one from John Tesh."
—DENNIS MILLER

Me, Myself, and I

During sex, I fantasize that I'm someone else.
—RICHARD LEWIS

I'm not offended by all the dumb-blonde jokes, because I know I'm not dumb. And I also know that I'm not blonde. —DOLLY PARTON

You know how it is when you go to be the subject of a psychology experiment, and nobody else shows up, and you think maybe that's part of the experiment? I'm like that all the time. —STEVEN WRIGHT

Everybody is a dork. Look: geek, weenie, twit, spaz, doofus. And it simplifies your life if you just admit it.
—SUE MURPHY

All your friends are like, "Hey, Dave, is that a bald spot or what?" "No, friend, it's a blowhole; I'm a dolphin."

—DAVE ATTELL

Anyone see me on the *David Letterman* show? Four million people watch that show, and I don't know where they are. But I believe it's a good introduction for a comedian. "You might have seen this next comedian on the *David Letterman* show," but I believe more people

have seen me at the store. Now, that would be a better introduction. "You might have seen this next comedian at the store." And people would say, "Hell, yes, I have!"
—MITCH HEDBERG

I don't have pet peeves like some people. I have whole kennels of irritation. —WHOOPI GOLDBERG

Do you ever find yourself standing in one of the rooms in your house and you can't remember why you went in there? And two words float across your mind: *Alzheimer's disease?* —GEORGE CARLIN

I never had a Barbie doll when I was growing up. I had a Tammy doll. She was like a Brand-X Barbie. You know, the doll that came with her own low self-esteem.
—CATHY LADMAN

We all feel like idiots at one time or another. Even if we feel we're cool 98 percent of the time, that 2 percent doofus is poised to take over our bodies without any warning. —ELLEN DEGENERES

I vent, therefore I am. —DENNIS MILLER

I love deadlines. I love the whooshing sound they make as they fly by. —DOUGLAS ADAMS

I just got back from Vegas. I was very excited. I was working the Riviera. The big thrill is to go out and see your name on the marquee. And I went out to look at my name, and it said, "Riviera . . . Sheila Kay . . . Craps in the Lounge." —SHEILA KAY

I read for the part of Elizabeth, the virgin queen. I thought they said they were looking for a virgin from Queens. Whatever, the only virgin in my house is the olive oil. —FRAN DRESCHER

If she'd stayed in England: If I'd have gotten really lucky, I might have joined the Spice Girls. I would have been Premenopausal Spice. —TRACEY ULLMAN

We're like the fatter and uglier version of Ben Affleck and Matt Damon. —KEVIN JAMES AND RAY ROMANO

I love Latin men, because they love cellulite and I'm their queen. —CAROLINE RHEA

We're all worms, but I do believe I'm a glowworm. —ROBIN WILLIAMS

Love me, love my farts. Love me, and know that periodically you're going to open the bathroom door and get killed. —WHOOPI GOLDBERG

Have you ever been talking to yourself and somebody comes in the room and you have to make believe you were singing? And you hope to God the other person believes there's really a song called "What Does She Think I Am, Some Kind of Putz?" —GEORGE CARLIN

I could never sell douche because I do not look fresh at all. I hate those commercials, anyway. I got so mad one day because I was watching TV and in the morning, I saw this woman and she was in a Monistat 7 commercial and that same day, I saw the same woman in an Always maxi-pad commercial. And I'm like, "Look, honey, I know way too much about your vagina." —MARGARET CHO

I toss and turn for hours until I realize that making salad isn't going to relax me. —GARRY SHANDLING

I am the worst driver. I should just drive a hearse and cut out the middleman. —WENDY LIEBMAN

When I'm on the road, I always have to have a good pen. If you've just got a Bic, they think you're on the skids. —BILLY CONNOLLY

Nothing wrong with being shallow, as long as you're insightful about it. —DENNIS MILLER

It's hard to be an individual among a billion people. That means even if you are a one-in-a-million kind of guy, there are still a thousand exactly like you.
—A. WHITNEY BROWN

I was in analysis. I was suicidal, as a matter of fact, and would have killed myself, but I was in analysis with a strict Freudian, and if you kill yourself, they make you pay for the sessions you miss. —WOODY ALLEN

I'm an actress. Just finished a play: *Twelve Angry Men.* It's a one-woman show. —BETSY SALKIND

My porn collection has never turned on me! It has never said no! It has been there for me under any circumstance, at any time of the day. Plus, I don't have to get it drunk to watch it. —ADAM CORROLLA

As you know by now, I'm Korean. I don't have a store or anything. Well, not anymore. —MARGARET CHO

I can't get into that California lifestyle. I was at the beach, and every time I would lie down, people would

push me back into the water. "Hurry up, he's dying."
—LOUIE ANDERSON

I don't have a fat body, I just have a really big head. I don't know how I'm going to lose weight in my head. What kind of crunches do I have to do?
—MARGARET CHO

I don't mind being held up as an icon of all that's wrong with television today; in fact, I'm flattered. I've worked hard over the years to make this profession more inclusive, by lowering the standards bar. —A. WHITNEY BROWN

If my film makes one more person miserable, I'll feel I've done my job. —WOODY ALLEN

> I knew I was an unwanted baby when I saw that my bath toys were a toaster and a radio.
>
> —JOAN RIVERS

I'm five foot five; please remain seated. My parents are short; I married a girl shorter than me; we're breeding down. We're going to be Shetland people.
—ROB SCHNEIDER

I watch the Weather Channel constantly. I am in love. Call me a geek, but I enjoy the enthusiasm of the Weather Channel hosts. I just enjoy it. I never knew anybody gave that much of a shit about weather.
—JON STEWART

One thing I hope I'll never be is drunk with my own power. And anybody who says I am will never work in this town again. —JIM CARREY

I noticed fairly early in life that some people live to find stuff to be indignant about. And it's pretty unattractive. That's why I decided to become a wiseass. —AL FRANKEN

I do not use any sort of consciousness-expanding material. My body will not tolerate that. I took a puff of the wrong cigarette at a fraternity dance once. The cops had to get me. I broke two teeth trying to give a hickey to the Statue of Liberty. —WOODY ALLEN

I understand why the doctor had to spank me when I was born, but I don't understand why he had to call me a whore. —SARAH SILVERMAN

Always look out for number one, and be careful not to step in number two. —RODNEY DANGERFIELD

Yeah, you so poor, you can't even pay attention.
—DAMON WAYANS

Spent the afternoon listening to self-improvement tapes.
Now I'm feeling a little inadequate. I don't have the
CDs. —DENNIS MILLER

To all those people who said my show wouldn't last, I
have one thing to say, "Good call!" —JON STEWART

The only resolution I've made this year is to stop worrying about all the little things that drive me crazy. I am
going to handle it when I drive through a McDonald's
and order a hamburger and some fourteen-year-old
asks, "Would you like French fries with that?" I simply
will say, "No," not "If I'd wanted the bleeping fries, I
would have asked for them, pimple face."
—LEWIS GRIZZARD

It's not easy becoming a stand-up comic. It's like becoming a murderer: No matter how much people try to talk
you out of it, you are going to do it. —JERRY SEINFELD

While awaiting sentencing, I decided to give stand-up
comedy a shot. The judge had suggested I get my act
together, and I took him seriously. —TIM ALLEN

People always ask me, "Were you funny as a child?" Well, no, I was an accountant. —ELLEN DEGENERES

It's not that I don't want to listen to people. I very much want to listen to people; I just can't hear them over my talking. —PAULA POUNDSTONE

Blondes have more fun, don't they? They must. How many brunettes do you see walking down the street with blonde roots? —RITA RUDNER

There is something about my personality that makes people believe they can be completely honest with me, and I hate that. —MARGARET CHO

Health

On exercise: At this point, at my age, it's just maintenance. . . . I'm just trying to stop my ass from going to Brazil without me. —SUE MURPHY

I hate the people who work at the gym because they're way too enthusiastic about life in general and about body-fat percentage in particular. I don't even know what they're talking about; they're like, "Hey, man, what are you gonna target today, your lats or your quads? You could work on your delts." "I'm gonna work on getting laid; that's why I'm here. Can you just point me to that machine?" —WADE FETTERMAN

What if I told the store clerk I wanted a basketball shoe and he asked how often I played and I had to sheepishly confess that the last time had been about two years ago and he sent me over to the shame section in the corner, where I was forced to purchase a pair of big, blue, fuzzy slippers with a swoosh mark on them? I couldn't risk it. . . . —PAULA POUNDSTONE

I look good? Lady, come on, I'm sweating like a pig; I'm prematurely balding; I'm screaming like a maniac. You could meet, like, forty guys just like me at the methadone clinic around the corner.
—BOBCAT GOLDTHWAIT

On the StairMaster: Folks, you want to go up and down stairs, move into a fifth floor walk-up on the Lower East Side. —DENIS LEARY

When I think about it, the only exercise program that has ever worked for me is occasionally getting up in the morning and jogging my memory to remind myself exactly how much I hate to exercise. —DENNIS MILLER

My wife's on a diet. She used to be so fat, every time she got into a taxi, the driver rushed her to the hospital. She went to the health club, and in one week, she lost fifteen pounds. One of those machines tore her leg off. —DAVE BARRY

How about when you're going up a flight of stairs and you think there's one more step? Then you kind of have to keep doing it so people will think it's something you do all the time? I do this all the time; it's the third stage of syphilis. —GEORGE CARLIN

I'm not into working out. My philosophy: No pain, no pain. —CAROL LEIFER

I once heard about a man who never drank and never smoked. He was healthy right up to the time he killed himself. —JOHNNY CARSON

If we listen to health food advice, all we would be allowed to put in our stomachs would be something animals graze on, bee pollen, and various sorts of bran. I don't know about anybody else, but eating a diet like that probably would make it necessary to spend a great deal of time in the bathroom, and I've other things to do. —LEWIS GRIZZARD

You know you're getting fat when you sit in your bathtub and the water in the toilet rises. —ETTA MAY

Red meat is *not* bad for you. Now, blue-green meat. *That's* bad for you! —TOMMY SMOTHERS

Now they can suck the fat out of one part of your body and put it into other parts. Boy, that's a bad idea. I want them to suck the fat out of my body and put it into Cindy Crawford. —RITA RUDNER

I'm starting to gain a little weight here because you live with a man, you gain weight. You know why? You starved your whole life to get one; you got one; you're going to eat now. —ELAYNE BOOSLER

You get very excited when they call you, because you think now you're going to see the doctor, but you're not. You're going into the next-smaller waiting room.

But now, you don't even have your magazine. You've got your pants around your ankles; you're sitting on that butcher paper they pull out over the table. Sometimes I bring a pickle with me and I put it next to me right there on the table. I don't know, in case the doctor wants to fold the whole thing up for a to-go order.
—JERRY SEINFELD

It is a good idea to shop around before you settle on a doctor. Ask about the condition of his Mercedes. Ask about the competence of his mechanic. Don't be shy! After all, you're paying for it. —DAVE BARRY

This warning from the New York City Department of Health Fraud: Be suspicious of any doctor who tries to take your temperature with his finger.
—DAVID LETTERMAN

I had to get an angiogram, and they shave your crotch, or maybe I just fell for it. They shave your crotch. And I'm scared to death 'cause they stick a tube in your thigh and feed it up to your heart. I said, "Is this going to hurt?" And they said, "No, don't worry. We're going to give you a little novocaine shot between your legs, and all you're going to feel is a little sting like when you're at the dentist." "What dentist do you go to?"
—ROBERT SCHIMMEL

Despite what Bob Dole says, I don't think the olden days were all that cheery. People had to have several kids to make a few of them take, people attended hangings for entertainment, your horse could step on your head, and doctors bled people. —PAULA POUNDSTONE

Just once I'd like to say to that doctor, "You know, I'm not ready for you yet. Why don't you go back in that little office and I'll be with you in a moment. And get your pants off."
—JERRY SEINFELD

Dentistry is the only branch of medical science that hasn't advanced in the last fifty years. There are no breakthroughs, no improvements. Technology has steered clear of the dental profession for many years.
—ADAM CORROLLA

Rhinoplasty, that's what they call it. Rhinoplasty. You've heard that term. Rhino. Is that necessary? The person obviously is aware that there's a problem. They made the appointment. —JERRY SEINFELD

I'm going to enjoy my coma. Hey, hell, I'm not paying for it. I've got family; I've got Medicare. Don't touch me. It'd be like having a government job. —DREW CAREY

You go blind, they ain't got nothing for you. You go to the doctor and tell 'em that you're blind, they go, "Hey, why don't you get this dog to drag your blind ass around?" What kind of cure is that? Where's the medicine? Where's the science? "I'm blind; I can't see! There's people that can see that can't handle a dog. Come on, gimme a midget or something!"
—CHRIS ROCK

Telling someone he looks healthy isn't a compliment, it's a second opinion.
—FRAN LEBOWITZ

If you are young and you drink a great deal, it will spoil your health, slow your mind, make you fat—in other words, turn you into an adult. —P. J. O'ROURKE

What always staggers me is that when people blow their noses, they always look into their hankies to see what came out. What do they expect to find? A silver sixpence? —BILLY CONNOLLY

Party responsibly; like, if you're gonna take drugs, sleep on your side so you don't choke on your own vomit.
—BOBCAT GOLDTHWAIT

I love to smoke. In fact, I love to smoke so much that I'm gonna get a tracheotomy so I can smoke two cigarettes at the same time. —DENIS LEARY

If you want to get one of those great red beefy, impressive-looking faces that politicians and corporation presidents have, you had better start drinking early and stick with it. —P. J. O'ROURKE

We have reached a point where over-the-counter drugs are actually stronger than anything you can buy on the streets. It says on the back of the NyQuil box: "May cause drowsiness." What it should say is: "Don't make any plans." —DENIS LEARY

It is better to be rich and healthy than poor and sick.
—DAVE BARRY

Yes, alcohol kills brain cells, but it's very selective. It only kills the brain cells that contain good sense, shame, embarrassment, and restraint. —P. J. O'ROURKE

I have the solution to the drug problem in this country. Nobody wants to hear it, but I have it. Not less drugs, more drugs. Get more drugs and give them to the right people. —DENIS LEARY

Every day I beat my own previous record for number of consecutive days I've stayed alive.
—GEORGE CARLIN

Eats

Cold soup is a very tricky thing, and it is the rare hostess who can carry it off. More often than not, the dinner guest is left with the impression that had he only come a little earlier, he could have gotten it while it was still hot. —FRAN LEBOWITZ

I'm learning to cook. I made a casserole. The only trouble is, when I wanted to take it out of the oven, I realized I don't even own any oven mitts. But luckily, since I'm a big sports fan, I had two Number One! foam hands. Which makes your casserole presentation oh so much more dramatic. . . . —SUE MURPHY

One time, I opened up a yogurt and underneath the lid it said: "Please try again." They were having a contest that I was unaware of, but I thought I might have opened the container wrong. Or maybe Yoplait was trying to inspire me: "Come on, Mitch, don't give up. Please try again, a message of inspiration from your friends at Yoplait. Fruit on the bottom, hope on top." —MITCH HEDBERG

Could we have some more virgin olive oil? This one's kinda trampy.
—ELLEN DEGENERES

Single women never keep food in the house. A single woman cannot sleep if there is anything edible in the home. "Okay, nothing to eat in here. I'm going to go lay down; I'll give it a shot. I don't know if I can sleep."
—ELAYNE BOOSLER

I had fried octopus last night. You have to be really quiet when you eat it. Otherwise, it emits a cloud of black smoke and falls on the floor. —STEVEN WRIGHT

Fish—you have to wonder about a food that everybody agrees is great except that sometimes it tastes like what it is. —P. J. O'ROURKE

A new report from the government says raw eggs may have salmonella and may be unsafe. In fact, the latest government theory says it wasn't the fall that killed Humpty-Dumpty; he was dead before he hit the ground.
—JAY LENO

Bachelor cooking is a matter of attitude. If you think of it as setting fire to things and making a mess, it's fun. It's not so much fun if you think of it as dinner. . . . Nomenclature is an important part of bachelor cooking. If you call it "Italian cheese toast," it's not disgusting to have warmed-over pizza for breakfast. —P. J. O'ROURKE

I saw a product in the market: Mister Salty pretzels. Isn't that nerve? Everything nowadays is low salt or salt free. Here's a guy, "The hell with you—Mister Salty pretzels" . . . like Mr. Tar-and-Nicotine Cigarettes, Mr. Gristle-and-Hard-Artery Beefsteak. . . . **—BILL MAHER**

Why is a birthday cake the only food you can blow on and spit on and everybody rushes to get a piece?
—BOBBY KELTON

The latest big thing is dolphin-safe tuna. That's what I noticed lately. That's the big victory, dolphin-safe tuna. That's great if you're a dolphin; what if you're a tuna? **—DREW CAREY**

Chicken of the Sea tuna. Theres no chicken in the sea. What are they afraid to tell us, it's fish? Afraid we won't understand? "Just put 'chicken' on the can. They'll think it's chickens that live in the sea." **—JERRY SEINFELD**

Men like to barbecue. Men will cook if danger is involved. **—RITA RUDNER**

Scientists don't know what's in tofu because even they are afraid to touch it. **—PAULA POUNDSTONE**

What is your hosts' purpose in having a party? Surely not for you to enjoy yourself; if that were their sole purpose, they'd have simply sent champagne and women over to your place by taxi. —P. J. O'ROURKE

People have been cooking and eating for thousands of years, so if you are the very first to have thought of adding fresh lime juice to scalloped potatoes, try to understand that there must be a reason for this.

—FRAN LEBOWITZ

That's a power meal: chili dog, bacon, cheese. That's the kinda meal that just marches down your throat. "Follow me, boys; we're going to the heart."
—DREW CAREY

I always get the dirty silverware at a restaurant. I always get that butter knife that looks like it was used in a homicide that afternoon, the one with the dried blood and hair on it. I'm trying to finish my meal, and Quincy's roping off the nonsmoking section.
—NICK DIPAOLO

Meaty Matters

There's only one food I won't eat, which is hot dogs at a movie theater, because I feel like there's no USDA preparation guidelines for this meat. They used to be impaled on spears rotating inside a Timex case. Suddenly that's gone and replaced by the foot massage–log roll jamboree. And they never look like they're cooking; they just look like they're sweating.
—WADE FETTERMAN

That Oscar Mayer section is creepy, too. This guy's inventing meat. There's no olive loaf animal as far as I know.

—JERRY SEINFELD

I think a rotisserie is like a really morbid Ferris wheel for chickens. It's a strange piece of machinery. We'll take the chicken, kill it, impale it, and then rotate. And I'll be damned if I'm not hungry! Because spinning chicken carcasses makes my mouth water! I like dizzy chicken. —MITCH HEDBERG

Bring me a live cow over to the table. I'll carve off what I want and ride the rest home. —DENIS LEARY

Currently, in the United States, 3.6 cans of SPAM are consumed every second. Prior to the birth of SPAM in 1937, 3.6 people stood in front of their open refrigerators, somewhere in the United States, saying, "I'm hungry for something and I don't know what," every second. —PAULA POUNDSTONE

Why does McDonald's have to count every burger that they sell? What is their ultimate goal? Do they want cows to surrender voluntarily? —JERRY SEINFELD

If I cut myself shaving, sausage gravy comes out. That's why I keep a pile of biscuits next to the sink.
—DREW CAREY

My father rationalized a fondness for pork chops by saying Mother's cooking rendered them unrecognizable by God. —MICHAEL FELDMAN

Despite the fact that meat is made from dead animals . . . almost all varieties of meat are good enough to be better than vegetables, except veal. Veal is very young beef, and, like a very young girlfriend, it's cute but boring and expensive. . . . Poultry is like meat, except when you cook it rare. Then it's like bird-flavored Jell-O.
—P. J. O'ROURKE

Vegged Out

A salad is not a meal. It is a style. —FRAN LEBOWITZ

Never trust a man who raves about fresh-cooked vegetables. —P. J. O'ROURKE

A vegetarian is a person who won't eat anything that can have children. —DAVID BRENNER

Tomorrow is National Meat-Out Day. It's being sponsored by vegetarians. Not exhibitionists.
—DAVID LETTERMAN

Most vegetables are something God invented to let women get even with their children. A fruit is a vegetable with looks and money. Plus, if you let fruit rot, it turns into wine, something brussels sprouts never do.
—P. J. O'ROURKE

If a man prepares dinner for you and the salad contains three or more types of lettuce, he is serious.

—RITA RUDNER

I just started eating health food. . . . I had an avocado-and-wood sandwich, and some pigeon milk. It was great. I went outside and went to the bathroom on the windshield of my car. —GARRY SHANDLING

I have a friend who's a macrobiotic. She doesn't eat meat, chicken, fish, white flour, sugar, or preservatives. She's pale, sickly, and exhausted just from looking for something to eat. She can eat wicker.
—PAULA POUNDSTONE

The government will be requiring new food labels that are more specific. Products will now be labeled "no fat," "low fat," "reduced fat," and "fat, but great personality."
—MICHAEL FELDMAN

The only good vegetable is Tabasco sauce.
—P. J. O'ROURKE

Today, we are urged to eat cereals with names like Nutri-Grain. Isn't that something they feed to cows out in Nebraska? And Fiber One. Sounds like a classification of racing cars. Then there's Product 19. And what happened to Products 1 through 18? Inquiring minds want to know. —LEWIS GRIZZARD

Any lettuce that comes from the store in a form that
can't be thrown from third base to home is too exotic.
—P. J. O'ROURKE

Going Out

I'm going to open my own restaurant with two smoking
sections: ultra and regular. —DENIS LEARY

We used to shoplift salamis when we were kids. You go
into a grocery store, you put one in your pants, and you
walk out, because no one's gonna stop you and go,
"Excuse me, is that a salami in your pants?" If they do,
you just go, "Thank you very much! I'm very proud of
it, myself." —GARRY SHANDLING

You've got bad eating habits if you use a grocery cart in
7-Eleven, okay? —DENNIS MILLER

Everywhere I go, I get hair in my food. I went to a
restaurant last week, two hairs in my soup, two in my
lettuce. The waiter comes out. "Can I get you anything
else?" "Yeah, how about a comb for the salad. What's
the house dressing, minoxidil? I ordered Romaine not
Rogaine." —NICK DIPAOLO

I went to a restaurant that serves "breakfast at any time." So I ordered French toast during the Renaissance.
—STEVEN WRIGHT

All the cereals nowadays: Cracklin' Oat Bran and Horkin Fiber Chunks. Cereals used to come with a free prize, now it comes with a free roll of toilet paper in every box. —DENIS LEARY

You know the sign that says NO SHIRT, NO SHOES, NO SERVICE? Does this mean as long as I have on a shirt and shoes, I can take off my pants and still get the bacon cheeseburger? —LEWIS GRIZZARD

I wake up in the morning and make myself a bowl of instant oatmeal, and then I don't do anything for an hour. It makes me wonder why I need instant oatmeal. I should get the regular oatmeal and feel productive.
—MITCH HEDBERG

Why is it whenever you go out to dinner with someone you'd really like to impress, you always leave the bathroom with a little piece of toilet paper still stuck to your tongue? —LAURA KIGHTLINGER

All this self-service nonsense began with the salad bar. Restaurants discovered people would actually get up and make their own salads. I've said it once and I'll say it again: I want somebody to bring my salad to me, because when I go out, I prefer not lifting a finger.
—LEWIS GRIZZARD

Bistromathics is simply a revolutionary new way of understanding the behavior of numbers. Just as Einstein observed that space was not an absolute, but depended on the observer's movement in space, and that time was not an absolute, but depended on the observer's movement in time, so it is now realized that numbers are not absolute, but depend on the observer's movement in restaurants. —DOUGLAS ADAMS

If you never saw a drive-through liquor store, this is what it is. I can't believe these things are even legal. It's a big-ass liquor store with a window on the side. Where you can drive up and buy Jack Daniel's, beer, whatever you want. While you're driving. It's almost a good idea. Just the thing for that drunk driver who's constantly on the go. —DREW CAREY

Uh-Oh, the Places You'll Go

Sometimes the road less traveled is less traveled for a reason. —JERRY SEINFELD

Here's a little tip from me to you as an experienced traveler. Wake-up calls: worst way to wake up. The phone rings; it's loud; you can't turn it down. I leave the number of the room next to me, and then it just rings kind of quiet, and you hear a guy yell, "What are you calling me for?" Then you get up and take a shower. It's great. —GARRY SHANDLING

As my good friend Al Capp told me a few years ago, the best thing to do with a confirmed [hotel] reservation slip when you have no room is to spread it out on the sidewalk in front of the hotel and go to sleep on it. You'll either embarrass the hotel into giving you a room or you'll be hauled off to the local jug, where at least you'll have a roof over your head. —ART BUCHWALD

Have you ever tried to sleep in a hotel with the air conditioner on high? Wake up the next morning, it's two degrees in your room. You got Walt Disney laying next to you. . . . Either that or they pump that real dry heat into your room. You wake up the next morning and the inside of your nose is like a box of Triscuits.
—NICK DIPAOLO

People lose their senses at the beach 'cause the sun beats down too hard. They say things that just don't jell, you know. Well, you've heard this a lot: "Pick up a shell, you can hear the ocean." You can pick up a bicycle and hear the ocean—you're at the beach. It's just your other ear, you know. Put the shell down. You'll hear the ocean twice as loud. —ELAYNE BOOSLER

To me, the outdoors is what you must pass through in order to get from your apartment into a taxicab. —FRAN LEBOWITZ

Never trust anything you read in a travel article. Travel articles appear in publications that sell large, expensive advertisements to tourism-related industries, and these industries do not wish to see articles with headlines like: "Uruguay: Don't Bother." —DAVE BARRY

We need an enemy closer to home. We're up there thousands and thousands of miles away bombing people. Why? Canada's right here! They're just waiting for us. We could drive up to the border and just throw it over. They don't even have an army, just two guys on horseback. —JON STEWART

There are two seasons in Scotland: June and winter. —BILLY CONNOLLY

You can always reason with a German. You can always reason with a barnyard animal, too, for all the good it does. —P. J. O'ROURKE

I understand that many women in Europe don't shave, but for the energy it would take me to learn another language, it's just not worth it. I'd be constantly flipping quickly through my Berlitz book to bumble out, "I certainly enjoyed not shaving today in your lovely city," to a native stranger over some sort of foamy coffee beverage. —PAULA POUNDSTONE

The French are sawed-off sissies who eat snails and slugs and cheese that smells like people's feet. Utter cowards who force their own children to drink wine, they gibber like baboons even when you try to speak to them in their own wimpy language. —P. J. O'ROURKE

I spent a couple of months in Paris. I lived in a really rough neighborhood, on a little street called Rue the Day. —DENNIS MILLER

In Montreal, in the French-speaking quarter, they treat Americans like shit, and you know why? Because years ago, they gave us the croissant. Le croissant. And what did we do? We turned it into the Croissan'wich, thank you very much. —DENIS LEARY

I think the Europeans are hostile toward the English because the English have some irritating habits—the habit, for instance, of ending sentences with questions that sound like reprimands: "You say it's difficult for you to tell because you haven't read the survey? Well, you'll have to read it, then, won't you?" See how snotty that sounds? —CALVIN TRILLIN

Nothing good has come from Switzerland: cuckoo clocks and Toblerone. It's impossible to eat a Toblerone without hurting yourself. —BILLY CONNOLLY

According to a new study from Italy, some women are actually able to hear with their breasts. Of course, this is great for Italian men, because they talk with their hands. —JAY LENO

I just got back from the Vatican. Kind of disillusioning. They had a Hard Rock. —DENNIS MILLER

Scottish Americans tell you that if you want to identify tartans, it's easy. You look under the kilt, and if it's a quarter-pounder, you know it's a McDonald's. —BILLY CONNOLLY

Why do the English talk so funny? For one thing, they're all hard of hearing. All Englishmen are hard of hearing. That's why they end a lot of sentences with questions just to check and make sure the other fellow heard what they were saying. . . . That's why they're always saying, "I say!" —CALVIN TRILLIN

What is it about Irish immigrants and paneling, does anybody know? We had paneling on the ceiling, on the floor; my mother had a dress made out of paneling. It's like they get off the boat at Ellis Island and say, "Forget about that freedom of speech. All we want is that . . . paneling; that's what we want." —DENIS LEARY

I've always wanted to go to Switzerland to see what the army does with those wee red knives.
—BILLY CONNOLLY

An anthropologist at Tulane has just come back from a field trip to New Guinea with reports of a tribe so primitive that they have Tide but not new Tide with lemon-fresh borax. —DAVID LETTERMAN

Americans are broad-minded people. They'll accept the fact that a person can be an alcoholic, a dope fiend, a wife beater, and even a newspaperman, but if a man doesn't drive, there's something wrong with him.
—ART BUCHWALD

I was raised in a small town, and I still remember every street. I knew it like the back of my father's hand. We were poor, but it didn't matter. We would have been just as miserable if we'd had money.
—A. WHITNEY BROWN

How about those people in Hawaii who build their homes next to an active volcano and then wonder why they have lava in their living rooms? —GEORGE CARLIN

I brought my wife with me to Las Vegas. You know how you pack a lot of things you don't need. —DAVE BARRY

Hate Cleveland in the winter. Nobody likes Cleveland in the winter—it's too cold. All I want to know is where the hell is all that global warming we've been hearing so much about? That's all I do here in the winter is stand outside with an aerosol can. That's right; screw the grandkids—I'm cold now. —DREW CAREY

Amtrak is unveiling a European-style rail line that links Eugene, Oregon, and Seattle, Washington. Within a month after opening the high-speed line, the population of Eugene is expected to be zero. —COLIN QUINN

When you step off the plane in Dallas and enter the main terminal, you are greeted by a huge sign that proudly proclaims: WELCOME TO DALLAS. WE HAVEN'T HAD AN ASSASSINATION IN OVER THIRTY YEARS! —AL FRANKEN

I used to love coming to Miami in my old carousing days, because of the Latino women. I loved getting rejected by women I couldn't even understand.
—JON STEWART

I understand that whole African American thing. Some black people just want to get in touch with their African roots. That's what they want to do, trying to find their African roots. But then there's some black people that just don't give a damn. You tell them, "Hey, I just got back from the motherland," and they like, "Where'd you go, Detroit? Did you see the Temptations?"
—WANDA SYKES-HALL

In Washington, D.C., public school officials are asking parents to pay for needed equipment, such as a new state-of-the-art surveillance system that one area school has requested. According to the school's principal, the new system will help him monitor cheerleaders he claims like to vandalize school property while showering.
—NORM MACDONALD

I used to live in Ohio for three years. It was a very small town, four thousand and five hundred people. My house was the black neighborhood. —DAVE CHAPPELLE

A new study listed the cities with the most cases of syphilis and gonorrhea. . . . New York wasn't even in the top twenty. New York's murder rate is down. Times Square is family-friendly. New York has become your crazy drinking buddy who got married and had kids. —COLIN QUINN

According to the *Rand McNally Places-Rated Almanac,* the best place to live in America is the city of Pittsburgh. The city of New York came in twenty-fifth. Here in New York, we really don't care too much. Because we know that we could beat up their city anytime. —DAVID LETTERMAN

According to a recent poll, half of New Yorkers say they would never move out of the city. Mostly because their probation won't allow it. —CONAN O'BRIEN

New York City's had kind of a tough summer. The people from *Roget's Thesaurus* announced that in their next edition, *New York City* will be listed for the first time officially as a synonym for *hell.* —DAVID LETTERMAN

Tourists, have some fun with New York's hard-boiled cabbies. When you get to your destination, say to your driver, "Pay? I was hitchhiking." —DAVID LETTERMAN

I moved. I formerly lived in Manhattan, uptown, but I was constantly getting mugged and assaulted. Sadistically beaten about the face and neck. So I moved into a door-manned apartment house on Park Avenue that's rich and secure and expensive. And I lived there for two weeks, and my doorman attacked me.
—WOODY ALLEN

I lived in New York, and I got a write-up in the *Village Voice,* and the writer really liked my show, and he was very, very complimentary, but he described me this way: "Funny, sexy, zaftig, Margaret Cho." What is zaftig? Isn't that German for big fat pig?
—MARGARET CHO

I love being in New York, I love running the bum gauntlet down every street. God, I hate those guys, man. The very idea they want me to give them the hard-earned money my folks send to me every week. Leech, get a job. My dad works eight hours a day for this quarter. I mean, the nerve. —BILL HICKS

New York parents are really upset because the Parks Department is building a beer-and-wine stand just twenty feet away from a playground. They're not worried about kids getting served alcohol, they're worried about drunk adults breaking the slide. —CONAN O'BRIEN

I live in New York City, and I feel very safe in New York City 'cause I've got that chain that goes from the wall to the door inside my apartment. I'll tell you what, you put that chain on at night and that just says to criminals, "Hey! You're not getting in here unless you push with your hand." —JON STEWART

Interesting survey in the current *Journal of Abnormal Psychology:* New York City has a higher percentage of people you shouldn't make any sudden moves around than any other city in the world. —DAVID LETTERMAN

I live in New York. I like New York; it's the only city where you actually have to say things like, "Hey, that's money; don't pee on that." —LOUIS C. K.

A New York hospital is replacing their cafeteria with a McDonald's. The best part is that the happy meal is 10 cc's of morphine. —CONAN O'BRIEN

In New York City, it has gotten hot and humid. Your strength is gone. For the last two weeks, New Yorkers have been giving each other only half a finger.
—DAVID LETTERMAN

New York really messes up your perspective, doesn't it? Even in little things. Like the other night, I'm watching that movie *The Diary of Anne Frank*. I used to have a normal reaction to that movie. I did—I felt bad for that poor family trapped in that tiny little attic. Now I'm looking at it and I'm going, "This is a great apartment. That skylight, that bookcase you go through, it's fabulous."
—FRANK MAYA

New York is now seizing the cars of drunk drivers, providing they can remember where they parked them.
—MICHAEL FELDMAN

I love living in New York. And people who live in New York, we wear that fact like a badge right on our sleeve, 'cause we know that fact impresses everybody. "I was in Vietnam." "So what? I live in New York."
—DENIS LEARY

The New York City Police now, they've got cops on bicycles. . . . I tell you, it's a little embarrassing when you get run down and arrested by a cop on a bicycle.

That's bad enough, but then you've got to ride all the way back to the station house on the handlebars.
—DAVID LETTERMAN

I love New York. It's the only place where if you look at anyone long enough, they'll eventually spit.
—CAROLINE RHEA

In San Francisco, people are so friendly here. I was on the cable car, and this guy offered me a seat on his lap. Then he got off. It was his stop. —WENDY LIEBMAN

If you're planning to travel to New York City, do yourself a favor—this is a lot of fun—check into a Times Square hotel. And take the Bible out of the nightstand there, if it hasn't already been stolen, of course. And open up to the Ten Commandments and go to the window, and on a good day, you can check the commandments off as you see them being broken.
—DAVID LETTERMAN

I went to San Francisco. I found someone's heart.
—STEVEN WRIGHT

New York . . . When civilization falls apart, remember, we were way ahead of you. —DAVID LETTERMAN

If you're going to write about disease, I would suggest that California is the place to do it. Dwarfism is never funny, but look at the result when it was dealt with out here in California: seven happy dwarfs. Can you imagine seven dwarfs in Czechoslovakia? You would get seven melancholic dwarfs at best, seven melancholic dwarfs with no handicapped parking spaces.
—STEVE MARTIN

In California, pet owners can now take canine friends to the world's first doggy wedding chapel, where dogs can be married in a civil ceremony, ending when the justice of the peace says, "You may now sniff the ass."
—NORM MACDONALD

Fall is my favorite season in L.A., watching the birds change color and fall from the trees.
—DAVID LETTERMAN

I moved to L.A., so I joined a gym, because it was either that or a gang, and I went with the gym.
—SUE MURPHY

The people in Venice Beach make the people in Times Square look like the Amish. —NICK DIPAOLO

Someone sent me a postcard picture of the earth. On the back, it said, "Wish you were here."
—STEVEN WRIGHT

The Unfriendly Skies

The Federal Aviation Administration has come up with a list of thirty changes to make air travel safer. Number one on the list: no more crashes. —NORM MACDONALD

I know that experts say you're more likely to get hurt crossing the street than you are flying, but that doesn't make me feel any less frightened of flying. If anything, it makes me more afraid of crossing the street.
—ELLEN DEGENERES

Airplanes are mass transit now, sort of skyborne Greyhound buses, but with longer lines for the bathroom and fewer chances of survival in a wreck.
—P. J. O'ROURKE

I just came in from the airport. My cabdriver smelled like a man eating Gorgonzola cheese while getting a permanent in the septic tank of a slaughterhouse. I said, "Hey, pal, there's an extra five in it for you if you run over a skunk." —DENNIS MILLER

I just love to fly. I love going in the airport. I feel safe in the airport, thanks to the high caliber individuals working in X-ray security. This Einstein has chosen to stand in front of X rays fourteen hours a day as his profession. I always look in the TV set; I cannot make out one object. I don't know what this guy is doing. He's going, "What is that, a hair dryer with a scope on it? That looks okay; keep it moving. Some kind of bowling ball candle? That's fine; we don't want to hold up the line. Don't hold up the line." —JERRY SEINFELD

"We would like to preboard those passengers traveling with small children." Well, what about those passengers traveling with large children? Suppose you have a two-year-old with pituitary disorder? You know, a six-foot infant with an oversized head. The kind of kid you see in the *National Enquirer* all the time. Actually, with a kid like that, I think you're better off checking him right in with your luggage at the curb. —GEORGE CARLIN

In order to cut down on in-flight fatalities, American Airlines has decided to upgrade the medical kits on all its planes. Each kit will now contain common lifesaving drugs, a heart defibrillator, and a spare plane. —NORM MACDONALD

It's, like, a million dollars to eat food at an airport. When did the airport become, like, the most expensive, coolest restaurant in town? "Oh, LAX; you must go." It's the airport; it's like playing *Wheel of Fortune*. "For $7,500, may I have the nachos, please? I was thinking about that home in Versailles, but maybe I'll just have the pepperoni slice." —BARRY SOBEL

Then I go in the bathroom at the airport. Now, I don't know who designs and makes these decisions, but why is it that we're not allowed to have actual twist-it-on, twist-it-off faucets in the bathroom? Is it just too risky for the general public to be in charge of the water flow? —JERRY SEINFELD

Lot of qualifications to sit next to that exit door now, huh? When did that happen? I've been a klutz, I've been sitting there, and nobody's said a word to me. I'm like Clouseau. All of a sudden I've got to be a Navy SEAL. —DENNIS MILLER

If the airport books are any indication, there are at least 450,000 evil Nazi World War II geniuses still at large, many of them with atomic laser cannons. —DAVE BARRY

The National Council on Psychic Research has officially designated this to be true: If you are passing through New York City and you must even change planes here, that counts; that experience of changing planes in New York City now officially counts as a near-death experience. —DAVID LETTERMAN

Then you get on the plane. The pilots always get to come on the P.A. system. Give you his whole thing of what he's gonna do. "Here's how I'm going to do it. I'm going to take it up to twenty thousand, and then I'm going to make a left by Chicago." We're all back there going, "Yeah, fine. Just do whatever the hell you gotta do. I don't know what the hell is going on up there. Just end up where it says on the ticket, okay? Can you do that?" —JERRY SEINFELD

Why do airlines put an oxygen mask directly over your seat? You don't need it there. You know where they should put it? Inside the tiny little bathroom. That's where you need the oxygen. —JAY LENO

Do the people that work in these little shops in the airport have any idea what the prices are anywhere else in the world? What do they think, that they've got their own little country out there? "Tuna sandwich, thirteen dollars. Tuna's very rare here." —JERRY SEINFELD

You're Not Getting Any Younger

My plastic surgeon told me that my face looked like a bouquet of elbows. —PHYLLIS DILLER

Went shopping today at the Mall of the Living Dead. I got stuck behind an 854-year-old woman at the bank machine, if I counted the rings correctly.
—DENNIS MILLER

Recently I realized teenaged girls don't even acknowledge me as a sexual being anymore. —MARC MARON

Right now I'm having amnesia and déjà vu at the same time. I think I've forgotten this before. —ROSEANNE

Going bald wouldn't be so bad if there were a reason for it, like a good reason. Like let's say under your hair, written on your head, are prizes. Like a scratch-off game. . . . "Hey, I'm bald, but look what I won, a large fries!" —DAVE ATTELL

I call them the lizard women. You know, the ones who have had so much cosmetic surgery, they're no longer biodegradable. They look like giant Komodo dragons with Chanel accessories. —BRETT BUTLER

A person over age sixty-five who drinks says that his doctor recommends it. —BOB SMITH

Middle age: when pulling an all-nighter means not having to get up to go to the bathroom.
—MICHAEL FELDMAN

I confess that when I first read that smog is particularly hazardous to children, senior citizens, and physically active people, for a brief moment, I thought, "I'm in the clear for at least ten more years."
—PAULA POUNDSTONE

As you get older, your health concerns change; they change so dramatically. When you're eighteen, do you even have health insurance? No, fake I.D., that's all you need. —JON STEWART

I don't want to achieve immortality through my work. I want to achieve it through not dying. —WOODY ALLEN

You know you are getting old when the candles cost more than the cake. —BOB HOPE

On Florida: I get very unnerved by the way they drive down there. That's why I don't like being in those communities. Because they drive slow; they sit low. That's their motto. The state flag should be just a steering wheel with a hat and two knuckles on it. —JERRY SEINFELD

You're not a kid anymore when you are obsessed with the thermostat. —JEFF FOXWORTHY

Perhaps I'm old and tired, but I always think that the chances of finding out what really is going on are so absurdly remote that the only thing to do is to say hang the sense of it and just keep yourself occupied.
—DOUGLAS ADAMS

On high school reunions: Don't go if you've never gone. You get that letter in the mail. You feel like you only have six months to make something of yourself.
—DREW CAREY

I just saw my grandmother . . . probably for the last time. She's not sick or anything, she just bores the hell out of me. —A. WHITNEY BROWN

According to a study, men whose wives nag them live longer. In a related story, next week, Frank Gifford turns eighty-six. —DAVID LETTERMAN

My grandmother used to say that she was pro-choice because she was pro-women. I think it was because she just couldn't see another generation borrowing money from her. —LAURA KIGHTLINGER

In Connecticut, Glastonbury High awarded Thomas Hennessy his high school diploma at the age of 102. Way to go, Thomas. In today's world, without a diploma, you've got no future. —NORM MACDONALD

I'm in my thirties. I went to the doctor recently 'cause I thought I had a hemorrhoid. What? It's humiliating to have to tell the doctor you think you have a hemorrhoid. Although apparently I have no trouble telling you people. —JON STEWART

Middle age is when your age starts to show around your middle. —BOB HOPE

Why not shoot the elderly into space? Stay with me. . . . Just think how many more manned space operations NASA could undertake if they didn't have to worry about getting the astronauts back. —AL FRANKEN

What is the age that old people reach when they decide, when they back out of the driveway, they're not looking anymore? You know how they do that? They just go, "Well, I'm old, and I'm coming back. I survived; let's see if you can." —JERRY SEINFELD

Here is God's cruel joke: By the time a guy figures out how women work, his penis doesn't work anymore.
—ADAM CORROLLA

It's been reported that the same chemical that makes disposable diapers work may help put out forest fires. Which is really good news for Florida, because most of its residents already wear diapers. —CONAN O'BRIEN

It's not that I'm afraid to die, I just don't want to be there when it happens. —WOODY ALLEN

Why have we always insisted on asking our young men, and now young women, in the flower of their lives, to risk themselves in combat? Why not use a human wave of our elderly to scare the enemy? What do these people really have to lose? The worst four years of their lives? —AL FRANKEN

You're not a kid anymore when you can live without sex, but not without your glasses. —JEFF FOXWORTHY

You know you are getting old when people tell you how good you look. —ALAN KING

How young can you die of old age? —STEVEN WRIGHT

Modern
Life

The good psychic would pick up the phone before it rang. Of course, it's possible there was nobody on the other line. Once she said, "God bless you." "I said, "I didn't sneeze." She looked deep into my eyes and said, "You will, eventually." And, damn if she wasn't right. Two days later, I sneezed. —ELLEN DEGENERES

Car companies are spending millions of dollars so drunk drivers can walk away from an accident. Why do you think drunks never get hurt? They're just as limp as the dummies that they're testing all year long.
—JOHNNY SANCHEZ

Whenever a heinous crime is committed, a newscaster will say that the criminal felt no remorse. Well, what could they say? "Damn, I just cut up ten people and shoved them down the toilet. I'm such an idiot. I'm always doing shit like that. I suppose they're all dead now, right? Oh, I could kick myself."
—LAURA KIGHTLINGER

Miniskirts caused feminism. Women wore miniskirts. Construction workers made ape noises. Women got pissed off. Once women were pissed off about this, they started thinking about all the other things they had to be pissed off about. —P. J. O'ROURKE

I don't know why people complain about secondhand smoke. At nearly two dollars a pack, don't they realize how much money they're saving? —DENNIS MILLER

I enjoy chaos and disorder, and not just because they help me professionally. —GEORGE CARLIN

There's this huge variety of Barbie dolls. They have Fun Time Barbie, Aviation Barbie. Oh, get this one: Gift-Giving Ken. You know, I really don't think this is going to prepare my niece for adult relationships. How about Date-Breaking Ken, I-Still-Live-with-My-Mother Ken, and Oh-You-Don't-Mind-If-My-Friend-Bob-Joins-Us Ken? —CATHY LADMAN

And, of course, you have the commercials where savvy businesspeople get ahead by using their Macintosh computers to create the ultimate American business product: a really sharp-looking report. —DAVE BARRY

They think we're dumb, so they put too many directions on products. Like on the home pregnancy test, it says, "For use in the privacy of your own home." Oh, good, I was going to drive to a crowded shopping center. —ELAYNE BOOSLER

Along with the standard computer warranty agreement which said that if the machine (1) didn't work, (2) didn't do what the expensive advertisement said, (3) electrocuted the immediate neighborhood, (4) and, in fact, failed entirely to be inside the expensive box when you opened it, this was expressly, absolutely, implicitly, and in no event the fault or responsibility of the manufacturer, that the purchaser should consider himself lucky to be allowed to give his money to the manufacturer, and that any attempt to treat what had just been paid for as the purchaser's own property would result in the attentions of serious men with menacing briefcases and very thin watches. —TERRY PRATCHETT

Martin Levine has passed away at the age of seventy-five. Mr. Levine had owned a movie-theater chain here in New York. The funeral will be held on Thursday, at 2:15, 4:20, 6:30, 8:40, and 10:50.
—DAVID LETTERMAN

I went down the street to the twenty-four-hour grocery. When I got there, the guy was locking the front door. I said, "Hey, the sign says you're open twenty-four hours." He said, "Yes, but not in a row." —STEVEN WRIGHT

Why do they call it rush hour when nothing moves?
—ROBIN WILLIAMS

I received an obscene phone call in the middle of the afternoon. A guy called and said, "I'd like to bite you, give you a spanking, and ride you till you beg for more." I said, "Thanks for the offer, but I've already got a long distance company." —LAURA KIGHTLINGER

If you ever watch any of these shows on, like, A&E, these biography-type shows, and they're talking about some guy around the turn of the century who was some politician, and he was a philandering guy, and then he ended up shooting somebody or something, they discuss it, and they say that for years, the town shunned him. When he came down the street, they walked on the other side of it. Nowadays, you cut your own penis off, you get a movie deal. —ADAM CORROLLA

Artificial insemination. That's a scary concept. You know why? I don't want to have coffee with a stranger, never mind have their child. —ROSIE O'DONNELL

Polite conversation is rarely either. —FRAN LEBOWITZ

When I get real bored, I like to drive downtown and get a great parking spot, then sit in my car and count how many people ask me if I'm leaving.
—STEVEN WRIGHT

The dumbest thing you can think in the back of a taxi-cab is, "Well, I'm sure the man knows what he's doing." Have you ever thought that? "He is driving fast and quite recklessly, on bald tires, but after all, he's a professional. I guess he does this all the time. He has a license. I can see it right there." I don't even know what it takes to get a cabdriver's license. I think all you need is a face; it also helps to have a name with eight consonants in a row. —JERRY SEINFELD

It's about time we realized nobody is happy. . . . Happiness comes in small doses. The five-second orgasm, the last chocolate chip cookie. You come, you eat it, you sigh, you feel guilty, you fall asleep, and you get up in the morning and you go to work. That's it, folks. Case closed. Final score: cookie 12, you 0.
—DENIS LEARY

The detergent Tide is improved. They are still working on Tide. —JERRY SEINFELD

I bet the "legalize pot" demonstrations would be fun to go to. That'd be all right. Probably last about five minutes and then just break down into a game of Frisbee or something. —JON STEWART

I get asked to do benefits a lot, and I've decided I've got to be a bit more discerning—I can't just do all of them. . . . I got asked to do a benefit for babies born addicted to crack. And I said, "Well, all right, I'll help you raise money for them, but I think we both know what they're gonna spend it on." —LAURA KIGHTLINGER

I've got some good news, if you're interested. They just opened a Starbucks in my living room.
—JANEANE GAROFALO

I went to a coffee shop here and found myself saying, "I'll have a large World Peace, iced." I'm still sick about it. What the hell am I doing here?
—LAURA KIGHTLINGER

On the Internet: It is an amazing communications tool that's bringing the whole world together. I mean, you sit down to sign on to America Online in your hometown, and it's just staggering to think that at the same moment, halfway around the world, in China, someone you've never met is sitting at their computer, hearing the exact same busy signal that you're hearing.
—DENNIS MILLER

The idea that Bill Gates has appeared like a knight in shining armor to lead all customers out of a mire of technological chaos neatly ignores the fact that it was he who, by peddling second-rate technology, led them into it in the first place. —DOUGLAS ADAMS

I am a happy nerd in cyberspace, where nobody can see my haircut. —DAVE BARRY

A lot of the success of daytime talk shows is due to the mentality of the viewers. I mean, if you put a TV show on during the time when people are supposed to be at work, think about your viewership! —ADAM CORROLLA

They always want you to be naked to get rid of stress; have you noticed that? To me, that's more stressful, actually. You know, you're naked, around people you don't know who are naked. You have no pockets. You don't know what to do with your hands.
—ELLEN DEGENERES

Computers make it easy to do a lot of things, but most of the things they make it easier to do, don't need to be done. —ANDY ROONEY

A Florida court ruled that exotic dancers must cover one-third of their buttocks. Now, if only they could pass the same law for the cable guy, we'd be in great shape.
—CONAN O'BRIEN

We shouldn't curse with sexual words. It gives sex a bad name in a situation like that. And it doesn't make sense; you're driving, someone cuts you off on the road, almost kills you, you roll down the window, wish them the nicest possible thing in the world. What is that? We need new curses, things that really mean something, things like, "Oh, yeah? Well, audit you, buddy!"
—ELAYNE BOOSLER

Reality is nothing but a collective hunch. —LILY TOMLIN

I also see in the coming year that there will be wars, and rumors of wars. Plagues and devastation will be visited upon the sons of man. And a child will be born in Bethlehem. . . . No, Detroit. Maybe more than one.
—A. WHITNEY BROWN

I can't use escalators. The banisters are always moving faster than the stairs. —BILLY CONNOLLY

So, do you live around here often? —STEVEN WRIGHT

Did you ever try to tell somebody they've got a little bit of dirt on their face? You can never get them to rub the right spot, can you? —GEORGE CARLIN

If you tell a joke in the forest, but nobody laughs, is it a joke? —STEVEN WRIGHT

I got in a fight with a really big guy, and he said, "I'm going to mop the floor with your face." I said, "You'll be sorry." He said, "Oh, yeah? Why?" and I said, "Well, you won't be able to get into the corners very well."
—EMO PHILIPS

If the shoe fits, get another one just like it.
—GEORGE CARLIN

I realize that I'm generalizing here, but as is often the case when I generalize, I don't care. —DAVE BARRY

The highway cop said, "Walk a straight line." I said, "Well, Officer Pythagoras, the closest you could ever come to achieving a straight line would be making an electroencephalogram of your own brain waves." I said, "Officer, I'm taking my mom to the hospital. She OD'd on reducing pills." He said, "I don't see any woman with you." I said, "I'm too late." He said, "You're under arrest. You have the right to remain silent. Do you wish to retain that right?" I thought: "Oooooh! A paradox."
—EMO PHILIPS

Tonight's forecast: dark. Continuing dark throughout the night and turning to widely scattered light in the morning. —GEORGE CARLIN

Why does that pharmacist have to be two and a half feet higher than everybody else? Who the hell is this guy? "Clear out, everybody; I'm working with pills up here. I can't be down on the floor with you people. I'm taking pills from this big bottle and I'm gonna put 'em in a little bottle." —JERRY SEINFELD

One time a cop pulled me over for running a stop sign. He said, "Didn't you see the stop sign?" I said, "Yeah, but I don't believe everything I read."
—STEVEN WRIGHT

I put that tooth under my pillow with dreams of a quarter in my head. I woke up in the middle of the night, and there was my father standing over the bed with his hand under the pillow. But I still believed in the tooth fairy. I just thought she had been there already and my father was ripping me off. So I bit him. The next night, I had two more teeth to put under the pillow.
—A. WHITNEY BROWN

One time a guy pulled a knife on me. . . . I could tell it wasn't a professional job; it had butter on it.
—RODNEY DANGERFIELD

First time I read the dictionary, I thought it was a poem about everything. —STEVEN WRIGHT

In China, do you think they call their good dishes America? —WENDY LIEBMAN

The future's so bright, I'm forced to squint.
—LAURA KIGHTLINGER

After they make Styrofoam, what do they ship it in?
—STEVEN WRIGHT

So what's with the cabdrivers and the B.O.? How long are these shifts? Do they ever stop, or do they just get in the cab and just drive until they're dead? Thats what it's starting to smell like in some of these cars. And then they have that cherry stuff, the cherry poppit on the dash. So you get the cherry B.O., which is supposed to be some sort of improvement, I guess. I don't know. I can't imagine even fruit going that long without showering.
—JERRY SEINFELD

There are some words in the English language, mostly detergents, that I think are Yiddish words. Like *Dreft*.
—MEL BROOKS

Let me ask you something: If someone's lying, are their pants really on fire? —JERRY SEINFELD

What's another word for *thesaurus*? —STEVEN WRIGHT